Sea Kayaking Illustrated

Sea Kayaking
Illustrated

RAGGED MOUNTAIN PRESS / McGRAW-HILL

Camden, Maine • New York • Chicago • San Francisco • Lisbon • London • Madrid •
Mexico City • Milan • New Delhi • San Juan • Seoul • Singapore • Sydney • Toronto

A Visual Guide
to Better Paddling

John Robison

The McGraw·Hill Companies

6 7 8 9 0 FGR FGR 0 9 8 7

Library of Congress Cataloging-in-Publication Data
Robison, John, 1966-
  Sea kayaking illustrated : a visual guide to better paddling / John Robison.
      p.   cm.
Includes index.
  ISBN 0-07-139234-3
  1. Sea kayaking. I. Title.
GV788.5.R63 2003
797.1'224—dc21   2002037100

Warning: Sea kayaking can take paddlers into harm's way, exposing them to risks of injury, cold-water exposure and hypothermia, drowning, and other hazards that can lead to serious injury or death.

   This book is not intended to replace instruction by a qualified instructor nor to substitute for good personal judgment. In using this book, the reader releases the author, publisher, and distributor from liability for any injury, including death, that might result. It is understood that you paddle at your own risk.

Questions regarding the content of this book should be addressed to
Ragged Mountain Press
P.O. Box 220
Camden, ME 04843
www.raggedmountainpress.com

Questions regarding the ordering of this book should be addressed to
The McGraw-Hill Companies
Customer Service Department
P.O. Box 547
Blacklick, OH 43004
Retail customers: 1-800-262-4729
Bookstores: 1-800-722-4726

⊕ This book printed on 60-lb. Computer Book, a recycled sheet containing 60% recycled content fiber.

Illustrations by John Robison
Author photo on page 1 by Elise Hughes

Contents

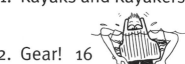

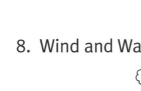

Acknowledgments

*I*t is very easy to underestimate the size and energy of the waves when standing on shore. It is also very easy to underestimate the size and energy of writing a book. Just like getting slammed back to the beach by the first wave of the set, making rapid progress on this book was not as easy as I expected. I had significant help keeping my momentum moving forward and keeping my pencil shaft vertical.

For getting me started in the first place, I would like to thank the following people: my mom, for encouraging me to go for the big waves; my sister Renee who signed me up for my first paddling trip ever; my sister Val for inspiring me with tales of Holy Kineenies; Jim Reid and Pierce Johnson of Woodberry Forest who taught me how to do my first kayak roll; Jim Lentz, Mike Woodruff, Alex Rabinovitch, and the rest of the Bowdoin Outing Club for many wonderful adventures; and Team Karma (Nazz, Flip, Scoob, Ram, Zeke, Atman, and the Daring Dipper) for all the moronic submergences.

I based the paddling techniques and rescues on the most current American Canoe Association (ACA) recommendations. Any errors are on my part. I would like to thank the ACA for their excellent series of classes and instructor development workshops. I would like to thank the following folks for sharing their teaching and paddling expertise over the years: all the instructors and staff at the Nan-tahala Outdoor Center (NOC) and California Canoe and Kayak (CCK). In particular I need to mention the master teachers John Lull, Debra Volturno, Kenny Howell, Marci Wise, and Shanna Holden from CCK, Jan Shriner and Roger Schumann from Eskape Sea Kayaking, and Greg Meyer with Great Expeditions. Ben Lawhon from Leave No Trace, Inc. provided excellent feedback on minimum-impact techniques. Matt Broze from Mariner Kayaks deserves extra special thanks for his outstanding editing. He crafts words with as much skill as he does kayaks.

Other folks who contributed tips include Geoff Harrison from the Boise State University Outing Club, Ben and Alejandra Gillam with Baja Outdoor Activities, Marie-Claude Tardif with Voodoo Kayaks, Nick Shade with Guillemot Kayaks, Chris Hipgrave, Esta Lee Albright, Thor Hanson, Bob White, David Lindsay, Joe Holland, Suzanne Meyers, Alan Peterson, Bruce Smith-hammer, David TeSelle, and Toby Fulwiler from the University of Vermont.

Thanks to Jon Eaton, Molly Mulhern, and the gang at Ragged Mountain Press for all their help in turning my chaotic piles of random sketches into a book.

Last but certainly not least, thanks, Elise, for being incredibly patient and supportive, but also for being the best paddling partner I could wish for. Now we can go kayaking!

Introduction

*M*y friends will tell you I can be a bit overly enthusiastic. Inevitably, subjects that I am keen about end up in my doodles. Take dinosaurs, for example. For the first ten years of my life, my artwork consisted almost entirely of dinosaurs eating other dinosaurs in front of erupting volcanoes. Later, spaceships, large-mouth bass, and giant tubing waves decorated my high school notebooks.

For the last sixteen years I have been particularly enthusiastic about kayaking. Whether you are skimming across a wave or poking around a marsh, kayaking is just plain fun. My mother was justifiably concerned about the direction my life took when I purchased my first kayak. After assessing my post-college career plans, she fatefully announced: "John, you're paddling to nowhere."

Hopefully my enthusiasm will leap out at you in the following pages. My goal is for this book to encourage you to get out in the water, take some classes and trips, and just muck around. That's where the real learning occurs. I hope you have as much fun looking through my renderings as I had creating them.

Kayaks and Kayakers

creek boat

whitewater playboat

sit-on-top

A kayak is any small craft that you power with a double-bladed paddle with your legs stretched out in front of you. When you put one in the ocean it becomes a sea kayak. Kayaks are amazing crafts with specialized designs for back-yard bayous, calm kelp beds, thrashy storm surf, and any other wet place. In general, the longer the kayak, the faster it is and the easier to paddle long distances. Classic sea or touring kayaks are expertly suited for multi-day open water expeditions because of their speed, cargo capacity, and unrivaled seaworthiness. Smaller-capacity day touring boats still have ample room to take gear for a weekend camping trip across the lake. Stable and predict-able recreational kayaks are at home

poking around calm lakes and bays. Tiny white-water playboats are slow but excel at gymnastics in the surf. Speedier surf kayaks are specialized for catching, shredding, and making sections on big glassy waves. Sit-on-tops can be designed to do any of the above without the worry of wet exits, and easy re-entry makes them the perfect choice for fishing, snorkeling, and diving. The tips in this book are offered particularly with touring kayaks in mind, although the concepts will apply to these other types of kayaks as well.

Types of Sea Kayaks

Each type of sea kayak is designed with a particular type of person in mind. Patterns become apparent if you look at people's interests beyond kayaking. Touring kayakers tend to enjoy backpacking, road biking, "backcountry" skiing, and their favorite movie is "Dances with Wolves." Surf kayakers like mountain biking, whitewater kayaking, and snowboarding and attend the Banff Film Festival annually. Folks in sporting kayaks enjoy fishing, diving, and hunting and love the "African Queen." Recreational kayakers spend time day hiking, car camping, cross-country skiing, and snowshoeing and watch the Discovery Channel. Some kayakers like to do all of the above and have several different boats.

20'

tandem kayaks
17'–23'

folding kayaks
12'–18'

boat length (longer usually = faster)

recreational kayaks
9'–16'

inflatable kayaks
9'–18'

sporting kayaks
10'–14'

7'

sheltered waterways

wave energy

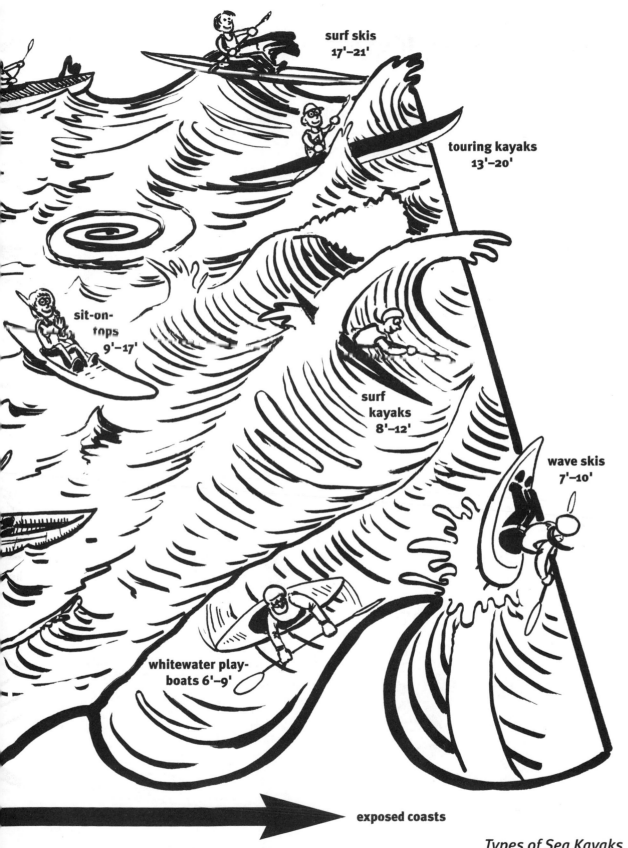

surf skis
17'–21'

touring kayaks
13'–20'

sit-on-
tops
9'–17'

surf
kayaks
8'–12'

wave skis
7'–10'

whitewater play-
boats 6'–9'

exposed coasts

Types of Sea Kayaks   **5**

Types of Sea Kayakers

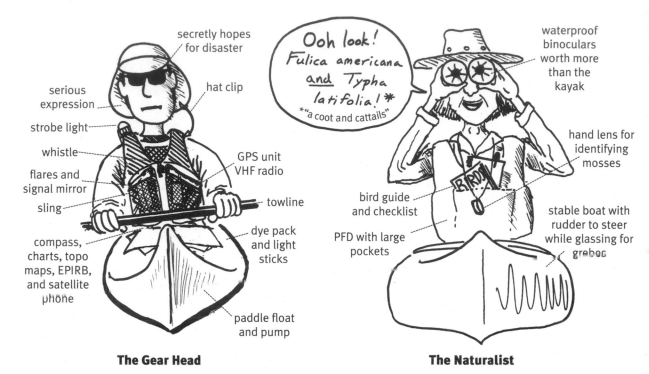

The Gear Head

- secretly hopes for disaster
- serious expression
- hat clip
- strobe light
- whistle
- flares and signal mirror
- sling
- GPS unit VHF radio
- towline
- compass, charts, topo maps, EPIRB, and satellite phone
- dye pack and light sticks
- paddle float and pump

The Naturalist

Ooh look! Fulica americana __and__ Typha latifolia! *"a coot and cattails"*

- waterproof binoculars worth more than the kayak
- hand lens for identifying mosses
- bird guide and checklist
- stable boat with rudder to steer while glassing for grebes
- PFD with large pockets

The Wave Hog

- playful wink as she snakes your wave
- nuggets of Mr. Zog's Sex Wax for paddle
- third-degree neck rash from drytop
- short nimble paddle for high RPM stroke rate
- neoprene sprayskirt
- highly maneuverable surf kayak

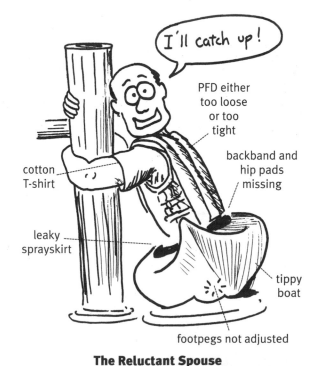

The Reluctant Spouse

I'll catch up!

- PFD either too loose or too tight
- backband and hip pads missing
- cotton T-shirt
- leaky sprayskirt
- tippy boat
- footpegs not adjusted

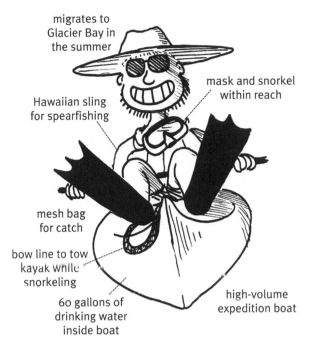

The Baja/Belize Bum

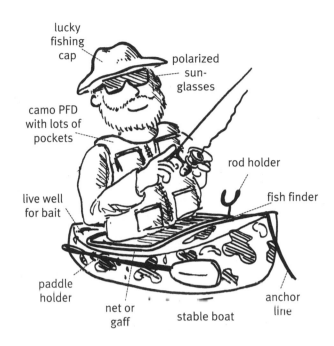

The Fishermaniac

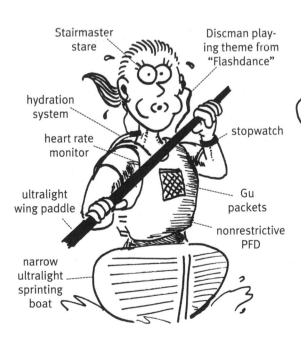

The Fitness Guru

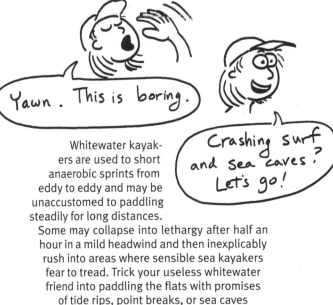

Whitewater kayakers are used to short anaerobic sprints from eddy to eddy and may be unaccustomed to paddling steadily for long distances. Some may collapse into lethargy after half an hour in a mild headwind and then inexplicably rush into areas where sensible sea kayakers fear to tread. Trick your useless whitewater friend into paddling the flats with promises of tide rips, point breaks, or sea caves just around the next point.

The Whitewater Kayaker

Kayak Details and Design

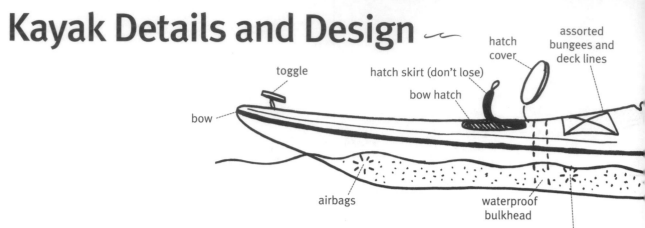

Most boaters have a vague notion that boat design is a precise science instead of a precise notion that it is a vague science. Anytime you talk with boat designers about why boats do what they do, they start throwing out caveats such as, "all things being equal," "there are no absolutes," and, "the tendency is." When two or three boat designers get together, they start fighting. While seaworthiness is the ability of a vessel to survive rough conditions, seawordiness is the ability of a kayaker to talk at great length about prismatic coefficients and stability curves, often to the annoyance of his or her

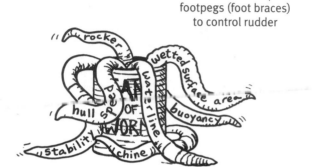

friends who just like to paddle. Here are some basic terms and generalities for which there are always exceptions.

Fish-form vs. Swede-form Hulls

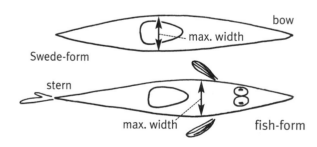

Two basic types of touring kayak are the Swede-form and the fish-form. "All things being equal," fish-form designs tend to stay on line or track better while Swede-form designs tend to be slightly faster and more maneuverable.

Bow and Deck Shapes

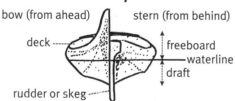

In addition to looking damn sexy, your bow should float over oncoming waves or slice through them and shed the water headed for your lap. The shape of the deck affects how your kayak responds to wind and waves, roll attempts, and two weeks of supplies. To add spice, stern decks are often shaped differently to minimize weathercocking, to carry additional gear, and to lessen the tendancy to broach in the soup.

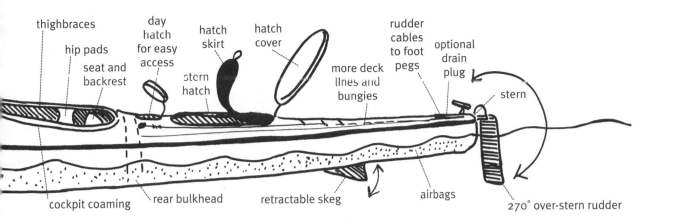

thighbraces
hip pads
seat and backrest
day hatch for easy access
stern hatch
hatch skirt
hatch cover
more deck lines and bungies
rudder cables to foot pegs
optional drain plug
stern
270° over-stern rudder
airbags
retractable skeg
rear bulkhead
cockpit coaming

Length and Width (Spud or Spear?)

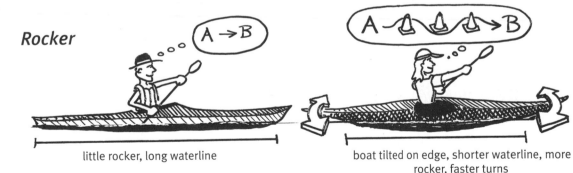

"spud": slow but stable, and easy to turn

"spear": fast in a straight line

The most important part about length is the length of kayak that is in the water, or the waterline. The longer the waterline, the faster the potential top speed of the kayak and the less maneuverable it becomes. Generally, narrow boats are faster and offer higher performance while wider boats are more stable. Use whatever makes the most sense to you. If you just plan on plunking around your backyard lagoon, skip the $3,500 graphite racing boat and get something comfortable that works for you and that you really like.

Rocker

little rocker, long waterline

boat tilted on edge, shorter waterline, more rocker, faster turns

How much banana is in your boat? Rocker is the amount of upsweep of the keel line from the middle of the boat to its bow and stern. A boat with a lot of rocker has a shorter waterline and thus less hull speed, but spins more easily and tends to keep its nose up while surfing. You can dramatically increase the functional rocker of a boat by tilting it over on its edge. Because kayaks are usually fattest in the middle, when you lean a kayak on its side you release the ends of the keel from the water, shortening the waterline and increasing the boat's ability to turn. Remember this when you need to turn in a hurry!

Stability

"Boats aren't unstable. People are."
— LINCOLN WILLIAMS

A subjective quality, primary stability describes how balanced the boat feels when level, while secondary stability refers to how balanced the boat feels when tilted. Stability is tied to the width of the kayak at the waterline, which changes as the boat tilts. The wider the waterline at that instant, the stronger the force pushing your boat back upright. Depending on the shape of your hull, the waterline may be widest at a tiny lean (good primary stability) or with a large lean (good secondary stability). Because a boat with good primary stability likes to stay flat to the water's surface, it is great in flatwater but horrible in choppy seas. If you do manage to lean It over you may not find much support. A kayak with good secondary stability may seem tippy in flatwater but at ease in rough seas. You can also easily edge it to turn and will feel at ease when there.

Chine, or What the Hull Is Going on Here?

Chine describes the shape of the hull where the side of the boat meets the bottom of the boat. Gradual or soft chines tend to be very forgiving but give snow saucers and kayaks a mushy feel when turning on edge. Abrupt or hard chines serve as directional keels and make snowboards and boats carve crisply, but are less forgiving if you lean the wrong way when crossing strong currents.

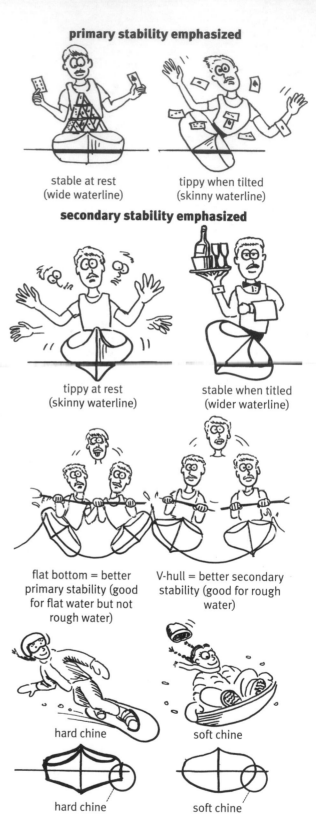

primary stability emphasized

stable at rest
(wide waterline)

tippy when tilted
(skinny waterline)

secondary stability emphasized

tippy at rest
(skinny waterline)

stable when titled
(wider waterline)

flat bottom = better primary stability (good for flat water but not rough water)

V-hull = better secondary stability (good for rough water)

hard chine

soft chine

hard chine

soft chine

Kayak Materials

Instead of asking what's under the hood (it's you!), you should ask what the hood is made of. The materials affect both the performance of a kayak as well as the ease of tansporting it.

Solid Hulls, or Hardshells

The stiffness of solid hulls makes them responsive but also harder to store in your closet or carry on an airplane. You have a choice between glass (fiberglass, Kevlar, or some composite) and plastic (polyethylene of some type).

Inflatables

Increasingly popular, inflatable kayaks are wonderful boats, particularly for beginners who don't mind going slow or getting wet. The carrying capacity and the performance tend to be less than kayaks with a solid hull.

Foldable and Collapsible Kayaks

somewhere on the tundra

meanwhile in Las Vegas

Folding, collapsible, or sectional kayaks are the way to go if you're going to be schlepping your boat on planes, trains, and buses to reach your destination and want a good performance boat once you get there. Their portable nature makes identifying your baggage of utmost importance.

Rudders

Crutches or Necessities?

rudder

no rudder

For someone just learning to paddle, a rudder can provide a short-term solution for steering problems, especially in side winds. If your mother-in-law is kayaking for the first time, place her in a kayak with a rudder. Rudders are rigged with cables to the foot braces. When you push one foot brace forward, the other foot brace slides backward, and your kayak turns toward the foot you pushed with (see Help from Your Hips on page 72 for a cool variation).

A rudder's real purpose is to hold your boat on a straight course in strong winds by keeping your stern from skidding out (see Weathercocking on page 129). Rudders are also helpful for steering lethargic double kayaks, but are no substitute for learning crucial steering strokes. If you depend on a rudder to steer and something goes wrong, you're literally up the creek. The play in a rudder system may also give your footpegs a sloppy feel.

Skegs (see page 9) are like retractable surf-board fins, and help a boat track but not turn. Because skegs do not move from side to side, your footpegs stay nice and firm.

Keep your rudder or skeg secured when transporting your kayak and when launching, landing, or moving backward to prevent it from hitting anything that might damage it. Learn to steer with your paddle and save your rudder for when you need help holding your course. When you lower your rudder, check to see that it is fully submerged, because the mechanism sometimes jams. The drag caused by a rudder cranked to the side can slow your kayak significantly and actually make it harder to turn. In the surf zone, a rudder can turn into an implement of destruction, so raise and secure it.

guillotine

peg leg

footpeg

Singles vs. Doubles

first date

last date

first anniversary

Singles are for doubles and doubles are for singles. Single kayaks are great for evenly matched couples. You have more independence and fewer disagreements. Two singles also carry more gear per person than a double.

Paddling a double is a great way to get to really know another person for the first time.

how tandem partners really view each other

Two people add significantly to the paddle power of a kayak, particularly if they paddle on the same side at the same time. It is also usually cheaper to rent a double if you think your relationship is up for the challenge. Avoid paddling tandem with a photographer, birder, or fishermaniac if you are not one yourself.

Pick the bow if you can maintain a steady paddling rhythm, like unimpeded views, and don't mind being a wind and splash shield for your partner. Pick the stern if you like being in control and know where you want to go. While it is possible to paddle a double kayak by yourself in calm conditions, it is slower and harder to handle than a single kayak, especially in wind.

typical photo taken by a stern paddler

When leading a large group, place people in double kayaks because it is easier to keep the group together. Double kayaks are also more stable than most singles, and tentative people can be placed with stronger paddlers to balance kayak speeds.

Tricking Your Boat Out

Your lower body should have several comfortable and snug points of contact with your boat. The balls of your feet should be braced against the footpegs, your knees secured under the thighbraces, your hips wiggle-proofed with foam, and your butt anchored to the seat with a Vulcan Butt Meld. Leave just enough wiggle room so you can stretch your legs by straightening your leg or slipping your knee out from under the thighbraces.

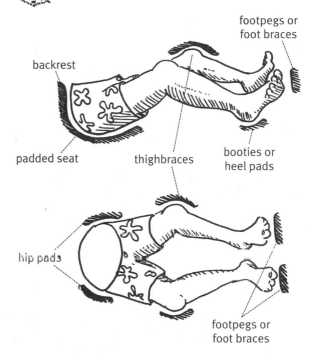

footpegs or foot braces

backrest

padded seat

thighbraces

booties or heel pads

hip pads

footpegs or foot braces

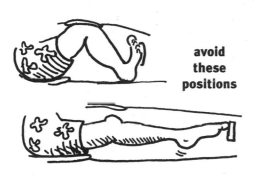

avoid these positions

Cockpit Modifications

The many systems available to help you bond with your boat range from inflatable seat cushions to gel-pack foot and heel pads. When gluing foam pads in your boat, use less glue and more ventilation than you think you will need.

Go to your local outfitter and see what foam scraps are available, then have an outfitting party with a friend. Convert a 4 x 6" block of foam into two hip pads by cutting it in half diagonally and then shaping the pieces with Dragon Skin.

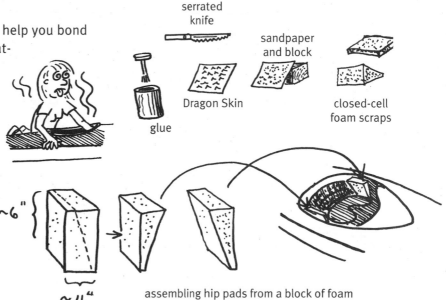

serrated knife

sandpaper and block

glue

Dragon Skin

closed-cell foam scraps

~6"

~4"

assembling hip pads from a block of foam

~ Gear!

*O*ur fascination with gear did not start with on-line shopping, but has been with us throughout human evolution. Humans are not just tool users, but tool droolers. Those ancient humans with fondness for the newest spear at the Outdoor Retailer Show were better hunters than their rock-throwing neighbors. This gear-head fascination helped pave the way for cell phones, ibuprofen, reality TV, Capilene, and the Exxon Valdez. Here is the newest (and already outdated) gear review of the five basic necessities and five hundred indispensable items for our sport.

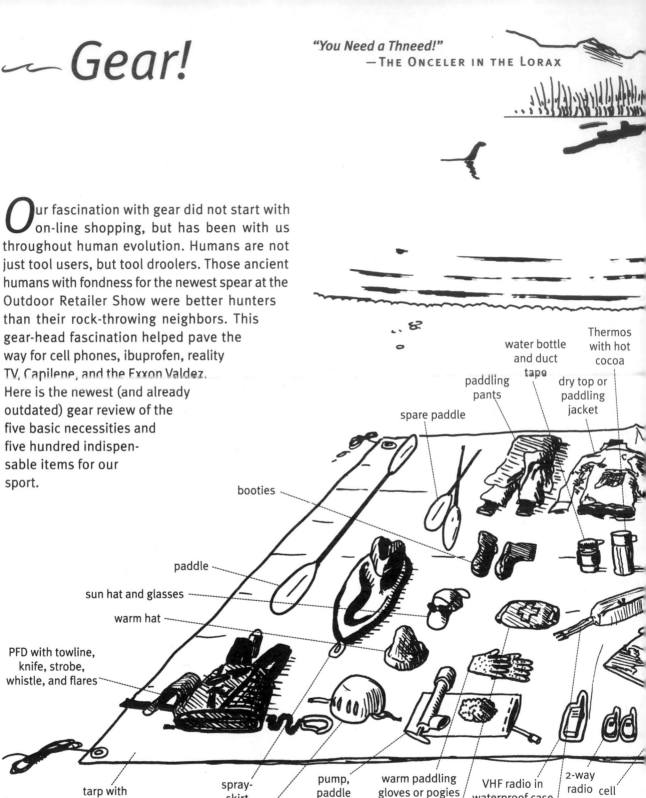

spare paddle

paddling pants

water bottle and duct tape

Thermos with hot cocoa

dry top or paddling jacket

booties

paddle

sun hat and glasses

warm hat

PFD with towline, knife, strobe, whistle, and flares

tarp with parachute cord

spray-skirt

helmet

pump, paddle float, and sponge

warm paddling gloves or pogies

first-aid kit

VHF radio in waterproof case

fanny pack with camp esentials

2-way radio

cell phone

16

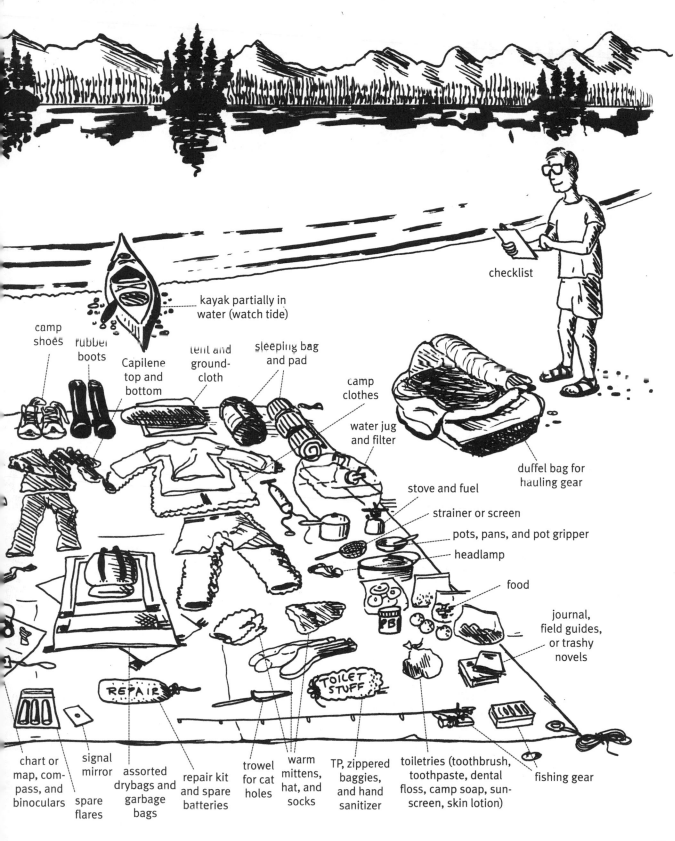

checklist

kayak partially in water (watch tide)

camp shoes

rubber boots

Capilene top and bottom

tent and ground-cloth

sleeping bag and pad

camp clothes

water jug and filter

stove and fuel

strainer or screen

pots, pans, and pot gripper

headlamp

food

journal, field guides, or trashy novels

duffel bag for hauling gear

REPAIR

TOILET STUFF

PB

chart or map, compass, and binoculars

signal mirror

spare flares

assorted drybags and garbage bags

repair kit and spare batteries

trowel for cat holes

warm mittens, hat, and socks

TP, zippered baggies, and hand sanitizer

toiletries (toothbrush, toothpaste, dental floss, camp soap, sunscreen, skin lotion)

fishing gear

Go Sticks! ～ *(Please Don't Call Them Oars)*

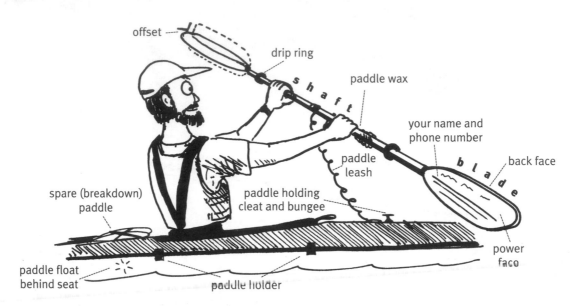

Think of your paddle as a magic wand enabling you to do wondrous things and move in mysterious ways. Paddles are more than aquatic ski poles. While many excellent skiers can get by with beater poles, your paddle is just as important as your kayak. Having said that, I lost several paddles when I was learning to kayak so you might want to hold off on that $400 paddle until your roll is bombproof. Remember to write your name and phone number on your paddle.

Length

Paddle lengths range from 245 cm for NBA players in touring kayaks to 190 cm for short shredders in surf kayaks.

Longer paddles help turn longer boats and provide a steady, energy-efficient stroke rate for cruising. Longer paddles also help you reach the water if you have a kayak with a wide hull, a high seat position like a sit-on-top. or a long back and short arms.

Shorter paddles provide fast, nimble strokes for precise maneuvering and quick acceleration common in whitewater paddling or surfing. A shorter paddle may also fit you if you have a short boat, a skinny hull, or longer arms that can reach out farther.

Blade Shape

A paddle with large (fat) blades is the equivalent of a pair of hiking boots with crampons, providing a lot of traction if you have the energy to heft them around. These paddles are well suited for anaerobic bursts of speed in surf zones or rock gardens. A paddle with smaller blades is like a pair of lightweight long-distance running shoes which require less strength to lift. These paddles are good for sustained aerobic touring throughout the day and offer less resistance against the wind. Symmetrical paddles are great for beginners who just want to pick up the paddle and go. Asymmetrical paddles are just as easy to use, but they have predetermined left and right blades to keep the blade from twisting and fluttering when it enters the water.

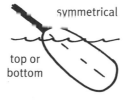

symmetrical

top or bottom

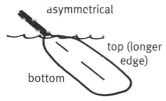

asymmetrical

top (longer edge)

bottom

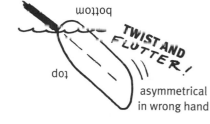

bottom

top

TWIST AND FLUTTER!

asymmetrical in wrong hand

Paddle Offset

The idea blade offset angle minimizes the need to roll your wrists yet is manageable in winds. The more vertical your paddle stroke, the more twist your body adds and the more offset you need to keep from rolling your wrists. Traditional Greenland-style paddlers who hold their shafts horizontally do not need any offset, while racers who hold their shafts vertically need offsets of up to 70° to *avoid* rolling their wrists. If you paddle a non-offset paddle vertically or an offset paddle horizontally, you will have to roll your wrists forward or backward, respectively. To slice through headwinds, an offset of 90° might seem ideal, but since this is far beyond your body's natural offset, you are forced to roll your wrists backward. First-time paddlers can start with a non-offset paddle for simplicity and then move on to a wrist-friendly offset near 45°, increasing to 60° for better aerodynamics if needed.

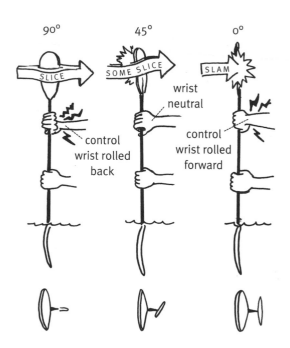

90°
SLICE
control wrist rolled back

45°
SOME SLICE
wrist neutral

0°
SLAM
control wrist rolled forward

Weight and Strength

Because you have to heft your paddle 500–1000 times to go just one mile, you will appreciate a light paddle at the end of the day. Lighter paddles are generally more expensive than heavier paddles, so go as light as you can afford. However, ultralight graphite paddles are more brittle so I recommend a somewhat beefier layup for surf zones, rock gardens, expeditions, and as a spare paddle.

Material

Space age composites are the best combinations of weight and strength, while wooden paddles win the aesthetic award and conduct less heat from your hands in cold weather. Test drive several types of paddles and select one you are stoked about.

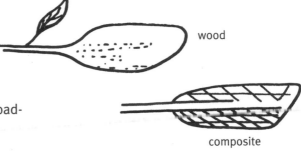

wood

composite

Paddle Shaft Shape

All paddles should have some type of oval oriented with the paddle blade so you can tell which way the blade is facing just from gripping the paddle shaft. This feel is essential when you are upside down in kelp. An oval paddle shaft also allows you to have a lighter grip when controlling your blade angle. If you have trouble with a round paddle shaft, create an oval by taping a pencil or thin dowel where your right hand grips the shaft.

Straight Paddle Shafts vs. Bent Paddle Shafts

Because the knuckle of your index finger is farther from your wrist than the knuckle of your pinky finger, your fingers grip the paddle shaft unequally. Bent shaft paddles conform to the shape of your hand and reduce the stress in your hand and wrist. Consider one if your wrist hurts and your bank account does not.

Paddle Accessories

Paddle Float

A paddle float is an indispensable item should you ever miss your roll or need extra stability. (See Rescues.) Stash it under your deck bungee or tether it behind your seat.

Spare (Breakdown) Paddle

Trick question: If you want to take a picture, should you set your paddle down on the upwind or downwind side of the kayak? If you said the downwind side because the wind blows your kayak faster than your paddle, you are correct (but you also flunk). You should never set an untethered paddle in the water because a loose paddle can quickly drift out of reach. Spare paddles are highly recommended for day trips and are necessities for overnight trips. Most spare paddles are breakdowns with adjustable blade angles.

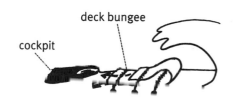

surf-resistant deck rig for paddle float

Leashes, Holders, Drip Rings, and Sex Wax

Paddle leashes and holders leave your hands free to cut bait or fish out other kayakers, but are not a substitute for a spare paddle. Attach the leash to your kayak instead of to yourself to keep the kayak and paddle together in case of a swim. Paddle leashes can become garrotes in the surf zone, so use them cautiously. When not needed, disconnect your leash from your kayak, roll it around your paddle shaft, and clip to itself to secure it.

Drip rings help keep your hands and lap dry. Surfboard wax such as Mr. Zog's Sex Wax can give you a better grip on slick paddle shafts in the surf. Use warm water wax so it doesn't melt and become ultra goopy.

Personal Flotation Devices (PFDs)

Outfitters don't like to say the word "lifejacket" anymore because of the legal irony if someone dies while wearing one. I like the New Zealand term "buoyancy aid" the best. A PFD is like a seat belt. If you wait until you need it to put it on, it's too late. PFDs are often thought of as Batman-like utility belts to which one can affix a dizzying array of gizmos. Remember that the primary function of a PFD is to keep you afloat, so make sure that these attachments do not interfere with your ability to paddle or swim.

The Need to Wear Them

Even when you think you don't need to wear your PFD (and you DO), other less-capable paddlers may watch you to see if they need to wear one. The Coast Guard currently allows kayakers to educate and regulate themselves, but it would take only another season or two of Darwin Awards about kayakers drowning with their PFDs strapped to their decks to change their perspective. Set a good example out there for all of us.

The Need to Adjust Them

A poorly adjusted PFD serves as a respectable substitute for a straitjacket, gag, and blindfold. Moreover, it is virtually impossible to adjust one when you are already in the drink. Tighten the straps after breaks and after getting splashed. If you can take full, deep breaths, it's too loose—and you need to tighten it some more.

loose foam

sun bleached

stuck zipper

torn strap

ten pounds of rescue gear

broken buckle

duct tape

classic guide PFD with zero flotation

The Need to Retire Them

Guides are notorious for wearing their favorite PFDs until the original color is unknowable. Retire your wave-weary PFD to the wall next to your Na Pali Coast photos. You can still show off your expertise through your stained and stinky lucky paddling hat.

Sprayskirts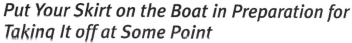

Here is where the sit-on-top folks just sit back and laugh. Sprayskirts are supposed to form a watertight seal between your torso and the cockpit coaming of a decked boat and are worn underneath your PFD. It is always better to have a skirt and not need it than need it and not have it. Coated nylon skirts may be easier to release and a little cooler in hot weather, but often form puddles and may implode if a big wave lands on your lap. Neoprene skirts withstand beatings in the surf better, but can be hot and restrictive when touring. To minimize leaks, wear a paddle jacket over your skirt or sandwich your skirt between the folds of your drytop.

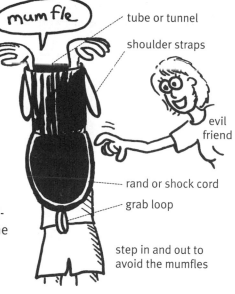

Put Your Skirt on the Boat in Preparation for Taking It off at Some Point

Start at the back and work forward, placing the grab loop OUT so you can break this seal in a hurry. If you have trouble putting your skirt on, wet it first and don't be the last person on the beach. Always check your friends' grab loops at the put-in to make sure they aren't tucked neatly and uselessly inside, making it difficult to wet exit.

Plan A. Use the grab loop.

Releasing Your Sprayskirt

While you can pop some skirts with your knee, plan on using the grab loop. Some folks clip a carabiner or ball to the grab loop so it hangs down and is easier to find with gloves on. First, use the cockpit rim as a guide to find your grab loop upside down in the dark. Second, push the grab loop forward toward your bow so the front of the sprayskirt clears the coaming. Third, pull the grab loop away from the deck.

If you can't find your grab loop and if lifting your knee doesn't work, bend to the side, press your palm on the skirt next to your hips, and stretch the skirt away from the coaming. Once you have a grip, free it from the coaming, and slide your hand along this opening toward the grab loop. Some skirts also have a tail of shock cord at the back you can grab. These options are preferable to the Scoober Maneuver, in which you wiggle out of the sprayskirt tube itself while hanging upside down in your boat. Practice a no-grab loop wet exit in a safe space where someone can spot you with an Eskimo rescue or a Hand of God.

Plan B. Open your skirt from the side.

Helmets

This topic is a no-brainer. Use a helmet whenever playing in the surf zone, rock gardens, or sea caves. Even in a sandy surf spot, there are plenty of potentially brain-damaging objects you could run into. These include your own paddle, boat, other paddlers, and surfboards. If you're not sure you will need your helmet, take it along just in case. It's always better to have it and not need it than to need it and not have it. Attach your nose clips to your helmet so you don't forget them and you won't have an excuse not to practice rolling. Wear earplugs in cold water to help keep your bony growths from sealing your ear canal shut over time.

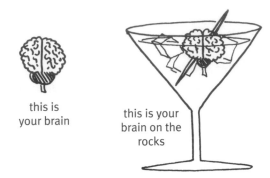

this is your brain

this is your brain on the rocks

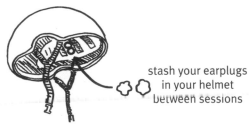

stash your earplugs in your helmet between sessions

Upside down in the surf zone

Ouch!

BRAINS! YUM!

Kayaking Accessories

A PFD for Your Kayak

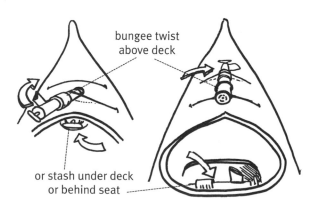

Watertight hatches and bulkheads, airbags, and sea socks are all intended to float your kayak should you become dislodged from it. These are not only safety items for you and your kayak, but for your friends who try to rescue you and your boat. Hatches and bulkheads need to be *watertight* to be effective. Make sure your airbags will not simply float away. Sea socks resemble bivy sacks that you secure around the cockpit and then sit in. They limit any water to where you are sitting. Drybags can also offer some flotation if they are secured. Back up your bulkheads or sea sock with a combination of airbags and drybags. You can blow up your airbags without undue dizziness by swooshing a garbage bag full of air and then squeezing the air into the open valve. Inflate them to fill in empty space around your gear and monitor them for leaks. They can pop if your kayak is on a hot beach or if you're going over a high mountain pass.

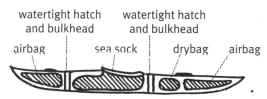

watertight hatch and bulkhead · watertight hatch and bulkhead

airbag · sea sock · drybag · airbag

swoosh

Water Letter-Outers

Sponges are great for dealing with leaky sprayskirts or overhydration mishaps, but are not effective for cockpits full of water. Bilge pumps are better suited for emptying a kayak full of water but take a lot of time and energy. Store yours securely on deck, under the deck with some Velcro or loops of shock cord, or behind your seat if you have good balance. Make sure it floats. To pump water in heavy seas without swamping, pump from a narrow gap between the side of your cockpit coaming and your skirt. Some plush boats come with built-in foot, hand, or electrical bilge pumps (particularly helpful for discreet peeing). Drain plugs are useful if you can haul your boat up on shore; remember to put the plug back in.

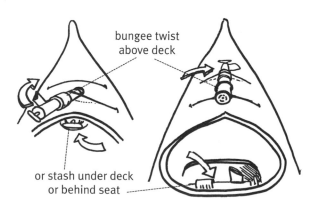

bungee twist above deck

or stash under deck or behind seat

Gotta lay off that coffee ...

Reflective Tape and Lights

Buy a roll with your friends and go nuts. Stick or sew strips to your boat, helmet, paddle blades, backpack, coffee mug, and PFD (beware of invalidating your Coast Guard approval unless you can peel it off). Keep appropriate lights at hand whenever paddling at night, but try not to use them and let your eyes adjust as much as possible.

Drybags and Deck Bags

In addition to providing some buoyancy should your bulkheads leak, drybags keep your TP in a usable form. The quickest way to check for leaks is to wear one on your head and look for daylight. Use a deck bag or fanny pack to organize useful items and minimize deck sprawl, but mount it where it won't interfere with your strokes.

Hydration Systems

How many times have you returned from a paddling trip with a full water bottle tucked inaccessibly behind your seat? Tube-style hydration systems that fit on your PFD or behind your seat make it easier for you to stay hydrated—and happy. A Thermos full of your favorite hot beverage provides significant comfort. Always secure water bottles and loose items with carabiners or mini-biners.

First-Aid and Repair Kits

Despite its convenient size, don't tuck your first-aid kit in the tip of your boat. A minimal repair kit should consist of a few yards of duct tape wrapped around your water bottle, a small tube of seam grip for gluing and patching, and a package of dental floss with a needle taped under the lid for sewing. Long wilderness trips should add critical spare parts, tools, and repair materials suitable for patching your boat.

"This ain't no raft trip."

deck bag

deck sprawl

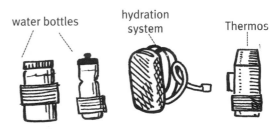

water bottles

hydration system

Thermos

"Duct tape is like the Force. It has a light side, and a dark side, and it holds the universe together." —GUIDE SAYING

Break out the duct tape and betadine!

Navigational Tools

Because it is hard to use parallel rulers in the surf zone, much of the course plotting happens the night before. Useful items to take with you include your chart and compass, tide table and watch, a course plotter and a waterproofed GPS unit with spare batteries.

Knives

Knives are handy for cutting tangled towlines, removing snarls of seal-strangling fishing line, as well as making peanut butter and jelly sandwiches. A blunt-tipped diving knife will also tighten loose screws and pry stubborn shellfish off rocks. Affix it so you can grab it with your dominant hand in one motion. Use a toggled cord to secure it in its sheath.

Weather Radios

Inexpensive shortwave weather radios help you avoid looking Perfectly Stupid in the next Perfect Storm. A computer-generated voice recites present conditions and forecasts for local areas several times an hour (you inevitably miss the information you need and have to listen to the entire loop). VHF radios (see next section) also pick up weather channels.

weather radio reception dance

Towlines

A towline is a must-have item for any trips where access points are few and far between. I am very fond of quick-release systems for unexpected situations or whiney towees.

Can't you go any faster - Hey!

Emergency Signaling Devices

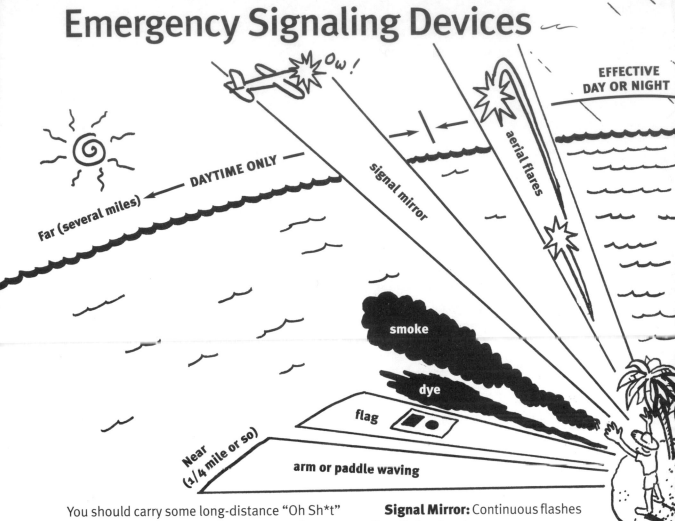

You should carry some long-distance "Oh Sh*t" signals to draw attention your way and some short-range "Over Here" signals to help rescuers find you.

Arm and Paddle Waving: Frantic arm or paddle waving is well recognized as a distress signal and should be your first instinct. Hold your paddle at an end to show you are in distress and not waving hello.

Smoke Canisters: Although limited to daylight and low-wind conditions, smoke canisters are a recognized emergency signal and should attract any boaters who see the smoke.

Dye Packets and Flags: A flag or cloud of dye is most useful when authorities have already been contacted and are searching in daylight by air.

Signal Mirror: Continuous flashes of sunlight aimed at passing planes or boats should prompt them to send someone to investigate.

EPIRB (Emergency Position-Indicating Radio Beacon): These beacons are picked up by VHF radios or satellites and are particularly helpful in remote or open-water situations.

VHF Radios and Cell Phones: Very High Frequency radios allow you to talk to other boaters within several miles along a line of sight. Channel 16 is the emergency channel and is monitored by many vessels and the Coast Guard.

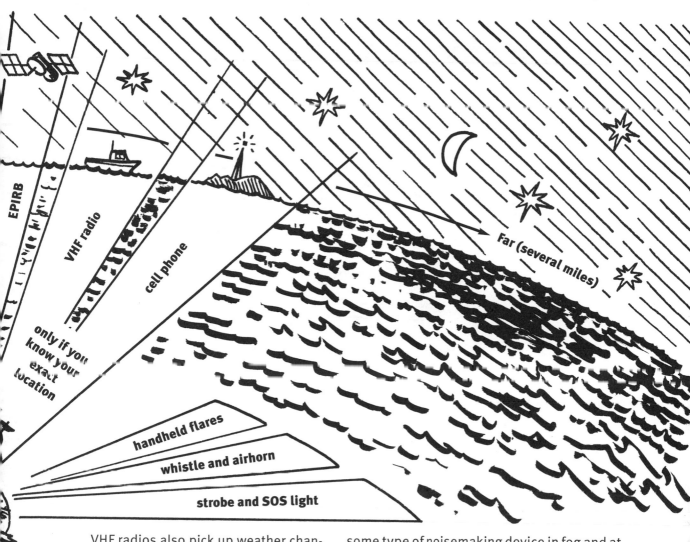

EPIRB

VHF radio

cell phone

only if you know your exact location

Far (several miles)

handheld flares

whistle and airhorn

strobe and SOS light

VHF radios also pick up weather channels better than most radios. A cell phone CAN be helpful in an emergency near civilization, but do not count on it as your only way of contacting help.

Flares: Flares will definitely let folks know there's something amiss and will draw attention your way (if anyone is there to see them). A set of three also complies with regulations for both day and nighttime distress signals, but you should carry spares. Check the expiration dates!

Tweet! Tweet!

You bought the cheap ones, didn't you?

Whistles and Air Horns: You should have some type of noisemaking device in fog and at night. Air horns are louder but whistles are simpler. Two short blasts every two minutes in the fog let other boats know you are out there so they can avoid you. A continuous blast is recognized as a distress signal and should attract attention.

Strobe Lights and SOS (• • • – – – • • •) Lights: In addition to serving as nighttime distress signals, these lights also comply with nighttime regulations and can be used to fine-tune a daytime search as well. Strobe lights are not official distress signals in international waters.

Nevermind. It's an O-S-O

Clothing for Kayaking

Dress for Distress! A fabric's suitability for paddling depends on its ability to insulate when dry, when submerged, and when damp. The key is the presence of an insulative layer that stays warm when wet. Seals use a wetsuit approach consisting of a thick layer of blubber, while sea otters and loons use a drysuit formed by air trapped in their dense fur or feathers. Good paddle tops are also waterproof and breathable, keeping you dry while rolling but allowing you to cool off when hot.

Welcome to Surfivor X! Meet Our Three Guest Paddlers:

The Cotton Kid, Capilene Carrie, and Neoprene Nellie are all comfortable in the warm, dry air, but that will soon change.

Meet She Moo and He Moo, two orcas that we trained to tip over their kayak.

Observe how all those valuable air pockets disappear on all but Neoprene Nellie. The Cotton Kid and Carrie are currently losing heat 2 gazillion times faster than before. Although Capilene and polypropylene are known for retaining their warmth when damp, they do not insulate very well when fully immersed. Cotton Kid and Carrie are going to be in trouble if they are not rescued soon! Meanwhile, Nellie has earned immunity and is feeling much more comfortable.

Now remove our group from the drink and see how they fare. While their heat loss rate has decreased dramatically, the Cotton Kid's clothes still offer no insulation and are in fact making him colder by holding water that is cooling him through both conduction and evaporation. Carrie's clothes have shed much of the water and have regained some insulative value, and Nellie is feeling refreshed.

After a two-hour paddle, the Cotton Kid has continued to lose heat and is now severely hypothermic. Carrie's Capilene has continued to wick moisture away from her skin, leaving her a bit damp but warm and comfortable. Nellie is stewing in her own sweat inside her wetsuit and she is in danger of overheating. Luckily, she can cool off by rolling, practicing an Eskimo rescue, or hopping out of her boat and taking a swim. If there's any chance of swimming, dress for the water temperature, not the air temperature. It is always easier to cool off than warm up! Capilene and a paddling shell is great if the water temperature is mild but you have to be 110% confident that you can roll or climb back in your boat in a few minutes in rough cold water conditions. Remember, kayaking is a water sport!

Layering Systems for Different Climates

Even in warm weather, bring an extra skull cap, swim cap, fleece hat, or neoprene hood. Lending a hat to a cold friend is the easiest way to prevent hypothermia in a paddling partner. In addition to protecting yourself from the cold, consider sun and insects as well.

	Next to Skin (wicking layer—optional)	**Insulation** (blubber or trapped air)
TROPICAL 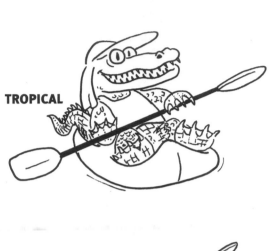	 ultralight synthetic	 surfskin or short-sleeve fleece
TEMPERATE 	 ultralight or lightweight synthetic	 medium-weight fleece
POLAR 	 lightweight synthetic	 heavy-weight fleece

If you don't have a bin, zip up your gear inside your PFD.

Outer Layer (waterproof)

shorty top or a long-sleeve nylon shirt for sun protection

dry top or paddle jacket and pants

farmer John wetsuit (no bottom fleece needed)

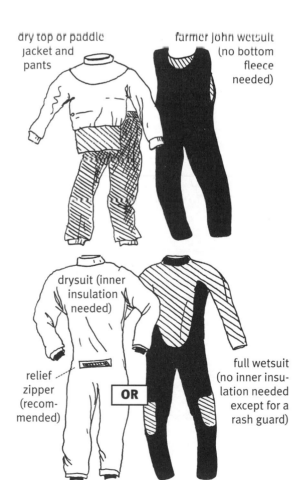

drysuit (inner insulation needed)

relief zipper (recommended)

OR

full wetsuit (no inner insulation needed except for a rash guard)

Extremities

paddling gloves (opt.)

sunglasses

sun hat

sunscreen

sandals

lightweight booties

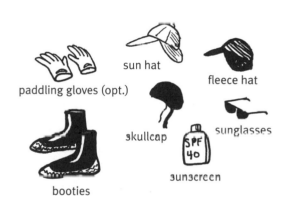

paddling gloves (opt.)

sun hat

fleece hat

skullcap

sunglasses

sunscreen

booties

pogies

synthetic or wool hat

neoprene gloves

sunglasses

skullcap

sunscreen

balaclava

neoprene booties

Pogies vs. Gloves ~ *Warm Hands in Winter*

Pogies are neoprene or fleece-lined mittens which wrap around the paddle shaft, allowing your bare hand to grip the paddle. Neoprene gloves act like a wetsuit for each finger. Unless it is cold, try paddling with bare hands. Any blisters should turn to proud calluses with time.

Pogies

Your hands cool quickly when they aren't gripping the paddle. Fleece pogies can also become wet and heavy.

You can feel the paddle and wield it more naturally.

A disadvantage is if you swim or lose your paddle, your hands have no protection.

Gloves

Your hands stay warm while putting on your sprayskirt and knuckle walking into the water.

Gloves make it harder to find the grab loop if you want to wet exit, so consider attaching something you can easily feel to your grab loop. It can also be hard to remove them to adjust things with your bare hands.

Your hands stay warm even while swimming.

Cold Weather Tips ～

Cozy Toes in the Cold

Sports sandals with optional wool socks are great footwear, but booties are better for colder waters. Zippered booties may be easy to put on and take off, but sand grains can jam the zippers in the open position, so use zipper-free booties if you spend a lot of time at the beach. In cold, calm waters rubber boots worn over wool socks can be useful for getting in and out of your kayak. Slip your boots off once you are in your boat for comfort and in case of a swim.

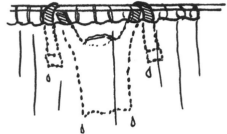

keep your drips inside the shower

Heating Hints Before and After Your Trip

To change discreetly, use the surfer's towel wrap and bring along a second towel to clean off your feet or lend to a forgetful friend. A dry Capilene top can lessen the shock of putting on a damp farmer john. If your wetsuit is sopping wet and you have access to warm water, soak your wetsuit in hot water just before you head out. Place the wetsuit in a cooler or a drybag to keep it toasty until you get to the beach. After your paddle, stand on a mat or in a plastic tub while you take your gear off to keep your clothes from becoming sandy. A jug of water is helpful for rinsing off booty spooge. Confine all your gear inside the tub to prevent salt water from completely corroding the inside of your rig.

drybag

towel wrap

bin for wet gear

extra towel for feet

fresh water to rinse off head/body/booties

shoes ready

mat

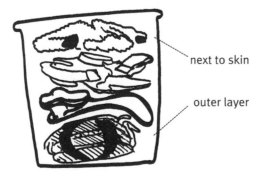

next to skin

outer layer

bin layered with gear for quick and easy changing

Carrying Kayaks

Or Hauling Things at High Speeds

"It'll be fine. We're only going a short way."
—EVERY PADDLER AT SOME POINT

Your first mistake . . .

. . . and your second.

To paddle a kayak you often have to carry it from place to place. You will need a vehicle (yourself, your buddy, a bike, or a car), a place to carry your kayak (your shoulder, a car rack, or a trailer rack), and a way of keeping it there (your hands, straps, or ropes tied in useful knots). Always empty your kayak as much as possible before carrying it.

Kayaks on Cars

Boats usually fit best right side up or on their side. If it rains, bail out your boat before the sloshing water bursts through your bow. If it rains frequently, consider carrying your boat upside down or buying a cockpit cover. Most paddlers believe that carrying a kayak backward is bad ju-ju. If you have an over-stern rudder, use a strap to hold it in place. If you don't have a strap for your rudder, carry your boat backward so the wind holds your rudder in place and knock on wood. Make sure that hatches and any gear on or in the kayak are secure.

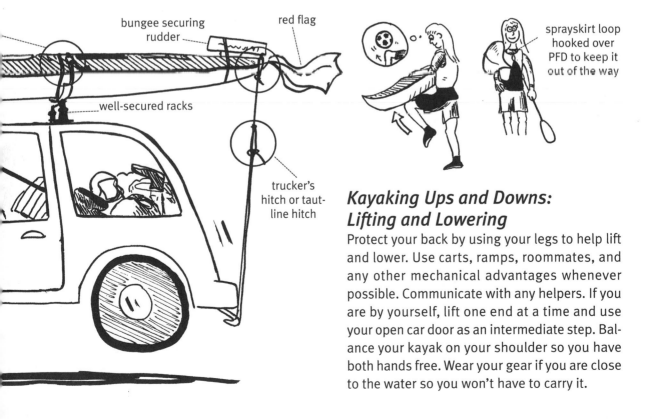

bungee securing rudder

red flag

well-secured racks

trucker's hitch or taut-line hitch

sprayskirt loop hooked over PFD to keep it out of the way

Kayaking Ups and Downs: Lifting and Lowering

Protect your back by using your legs to help lift and lower. Use carts, ramps, roommates, and any other mechanical advantages whenever possible. Communicate with any helpers. If you are by yourself, lift one end at a time and use your open car door as an intermediate step. Balance your kayak on your shoulder so you have both hands free. Wear your gear if you are close to the water so you won't have to carry it.

Knots for the Knotically Impaired ~

Now that your kayak is on your car, you want to keep it there. A good knot 1. is easy to tie, 2. holds, 3. is easy to untie. This section is designed to help you overcome your fear of ropes so you can impress the hell out of your paddling buddies who have long suspected you of being a knotless twit. There are many different ways to tie each of these knots. Start with more slack than you think you will need. Find the way that works best for you.

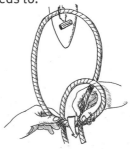

The Bowline

The bowline is your basic loop used to attach a rope to things such as grab loops, car racks, trees, or tents. A bowline (rhymes with "Oh Lynn") is the knot, while a bow line (sounds like "Ow, mine") is a line from your boat to your bumper. Practice by tying a loop around a table leg or lamp in front of you with the bulk of the rope behind you, as shown below.

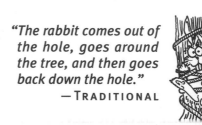

"The rabbit comes out of the hole, goes around the tree, and then goes back down the hole."
—Traditional

1. Make a T with the rope as shown. Remember to breathe.

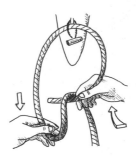

2. Move your right hand down and away from you and your left hand toward you. The rope will move as it needs to.

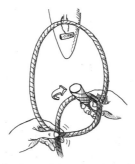

3. Give a thumbs-up with your right hand so the end is now vertical. Grip the rope with your left hand where it crosses, forming a loop.

4. Point the end of the rope toward you.

5. Switch your grip with your right hand so you can pull the end through the loop toward you.

6. Pull the end toward you. You are doing fine.

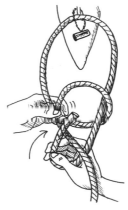

7. Move your right hand underneath the other section of rope and toward your left hand. Almost there.

8. Bend the end of the rope so your left hand can grab it and pull it through the loop.

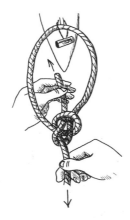

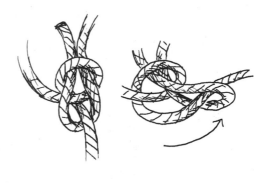

9. Tighten the knot by pulling the end away from you with your left hand and pulling the main section of rope toward you with your right hand.

10. To untie a bowline, find some slack and bend the neck over.

Trucker's Hitch

This is the ultimate knot for cinching your hull to the roof rack, securing your bow to the bumper, and for dragging your truck out of a ditch.

Tie one end of your rope to the bar with a bowline, toss the rope over the kayak, and pass it underneath the bar. Next tie a quick-release loop a foot or two above the bar by following these steps:

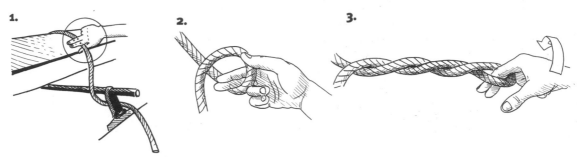

1. Grasp the rope between your fingers and thumb. 2. Twist your hand palm up.

3. Keep twisting the rope with your fingers until you form at least two full wraps. If you stop at one twist, the loop will become a permanent part of your rope.

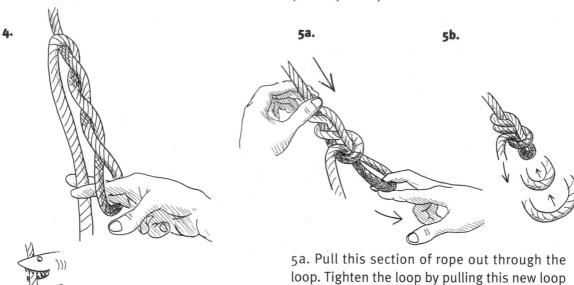

4. Reach through the loop with your two fingers and grasp the rope below your wraps.

5a. Pull this section of rope out through the loop. Tighten the loop by pulling this new loop down and sliding the wrapped coils down.

5b. To untie this loop later, pull down on the free end. The more wraps the easier the quick-release loop will release.

6.

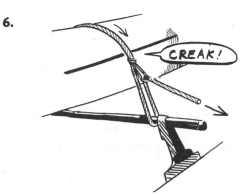

6. Bring the end of the rope up through this new loop, and back down toward you. Pull down on the end until the boat creaks, but be careful with fiberglass boats.

7.

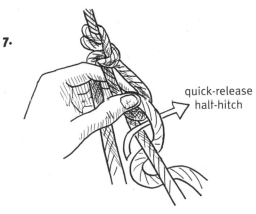

quick-release half-hitch

7. To maintain the tension, pinch the rope where it wraps through the loop. Tie a quick-release half-hitch with a doubled-up section of the free end.

8.

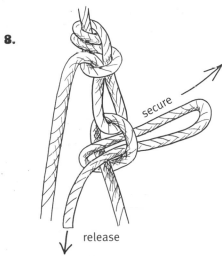

secure

release

8. Pull up on this loop to secure the knot or pull down on the free end to release it.

9.

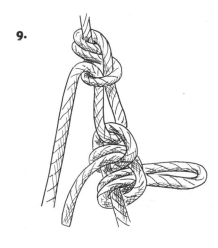

9. For a bomber finish, make one more wrap and tuck.

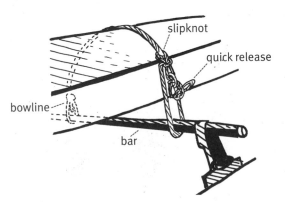

slipknot

quick release

bowline

bar

Taut-Line Hitch

Use this adjustable knot to tie a line from your boat to your bumper, to secure your tent fly to a stake, or just to tie up loose ends.

1.

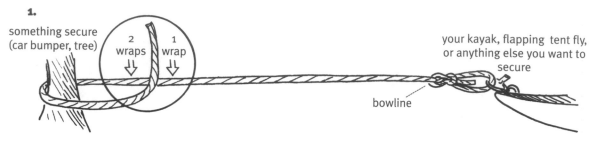

something secure (car bumper, tree)

2 wraps | 1 wrap

your kayak, flapping tent fly, or anything else you want to secure

bowline

1. First use your ubiquitous bowline to tie your rope to your kayak or tent fly. Then wrap the other end of the rope around a secure object and make a T with at a 2' tail.

2.

2. Make two wraps on the inside of the loop.

3.

Midshipman's Hitch variation

3. You can also bring the second wrap across the first one to form an X, a less-adjustable variation known as the Midshipman's Hitch.

4.

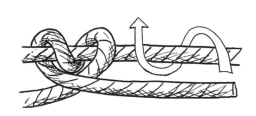

4. Next make one wrap on the outside of the loop. Tighten by pulling at right angles to the rope.

5.

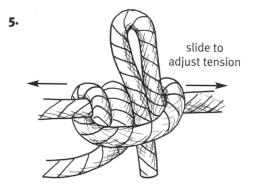

slide to adjust tension

5. To adjust, grip the knot itself and slide it up or down. To make a quick-release version, make the final wrap with a short loop. If you have a ton of rope and a short distance, tie this knot with a doubled section of line.

Clove Hitch

The clove hitch is simply a good knot for tying a boat to a piling or a tree.

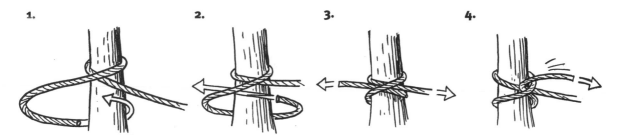

1.   **2.**   **3.**   **4.**

1. Wrap the rope around the tree so it makes an X. 2. Wrap the rope around the tree again and slip it directly underneath the X.

3. Now pull the knot tight by tugging on both ends. 4. Loosen the knot by pulling each end back across the center of the X.

Clove Hitch — Speedy Version

Use this version when you can reach over the top of a piling.

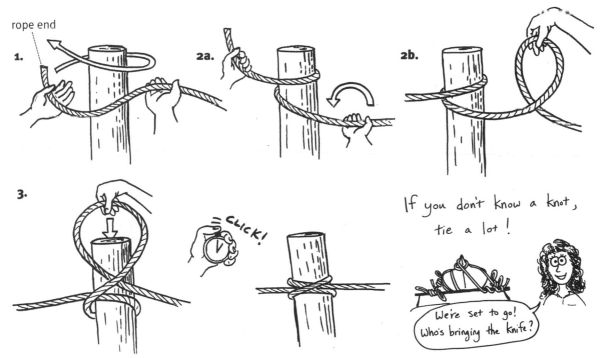

rope end

1.   2a.   2b.

3.

= CLICK!

If you don't know a knot, tie a lot!

We're set to go! Who's bringing the knife?

1. Hold the rope with both hands palm up. Wrap the loose end of the rope clockwise around the piling with your left hand.

2a–2b. Turn your right hand palm down to form a loop.
3. Drop this loop over the piling and tighten.

Figure 8 Knot

The figure 8 is a good stopper knot for shock cords because it won't roll off the end of the line.

overhand (lame)

The figure 8 is simply an overhand knot with one extra wrap in it.

figure 8 (good)

Figure 8 Follow-Through

Use the figure 8 follow-through to tie a semipermanent loop around something (such as an anchor) or to join two ropes of the same diameter.

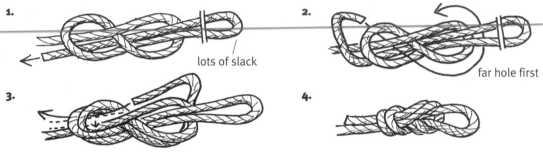

1.

lots of slack

2.

far hole first

3.

push line over and slip end through

4.

After tying a figure 8 with a long tail and making your loop, retrace the knot with the loose end.

Sheet Bend

The sheet bend is a quick and easy way to join two ropes together, even with different diameters.

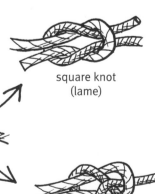

square knot (lame)

The sheet bend is similar to the square knot but is much more reliable. An extra wrap at the end makes it more secure.

sheet bend (rad)

Cam Straps

For rope-challenged individuals, cam straps are the solution. Straps are remarkably simple but some guidance can be helpful. If your cam strap sack looks more like a snake pit, take a few minutes to organize your straps.

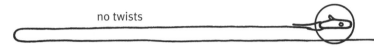

no twists

1. Find the midpoint of your cam strap and extend the non-buckle end about a foot past the buckle end. Be sure that the top of the buckle lever is facing away from the loose end.

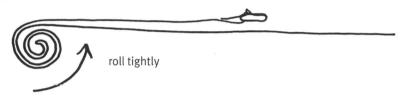

roll tightly

2. Pinch the middle of the strap and roll the midpoint toward the ends so it is underneath the buckle.

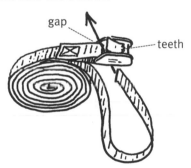

gap

teeth

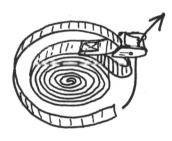

3. Once you have rolled to the buckle, slip the remaining 12" through the gap in the buckle behind the teeth.

4. Wrap this loose end around the entire roll, away from the teeth.

Gotcha!

5. Feed the loose end up through the teeth the normal way and cinch down.

6. Ta Da!

Kayak Jenga ⌁ *The Art of Arranging Kayaks*

I think the blue one is looser.

Whoa! Careful chief! You don't want to have to restack them again.

Remember, it has to stay on top for 10 seconds before your turn is over.

There is an art to arranging kayaks on racks. Scratch-sensitive composite kayaks do best on padded racks. Comfy kayak saddles provide the most suport for any kayak. Use vertical bars, or stackers, to prop a kayak on its side.

This put in can be a little busy.

Placing Your Boat
First, place your kayak on the passenger side to keep from getting sideswiped at the put-in.

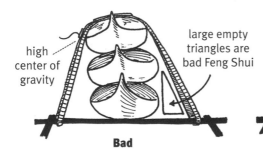

high center of gravity

large empty triangles are bad Feng Shui

Bad

Good

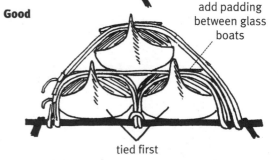

add padding between glass boats

tied first

Load boats as closely to the bar as possible so they can't shift any lower. A flat kayak or a kayak in a saddle can make a stable stacker for other kayaks. The other kayaks can be tied separately with straps over all the boats. A third boat can be loaded on top with separate straps.

The Good, the Bad, and the Ugly

Here are a few hints for securing boats securely.

Wrapping the strap or rope all the way around the bar is not as secure as cinching it down across the top from either side. An extra wrap around the bar will help keep the strap and kayak from shifting.

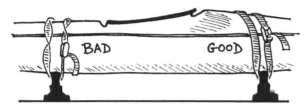

The fewer twists the better, although an occasional twist can eliminate strap vibrations at high speeds.

Clean and pointy ends feed through buckles more easily than frayed, blunt ends. Cut a new edge at an angle and carefully melt it with a lighter.

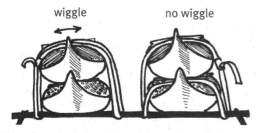

If you need to stack two plastic kayaks on top of each other, try the no-wiggle method.

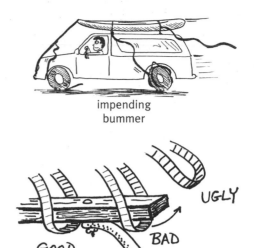

impending bummer

Run the straps *inside* the rack towers.

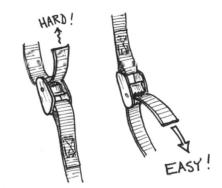

Place the buckles so you can pull down to tighten.

Secure a loose end by tucking it back under the strap or closing it inside a car door. You can also tie it off with a taut-line hitch or wrap it around the bar and secure it with a clove hitch.

The Girth Hitch Trick

What if you have two kayaks, two long straps or ropes, and no stackers?

1. Tied like this, the kayaks may shift, scratch each other, and fall off

2. To solve this problem, extend the buckle 4' or so past the loose end and put the center of the strap behind the bar.

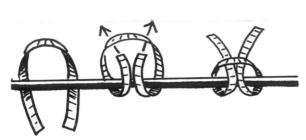

3. Make a girth hitch by bringing both ends in front of the bar and up through the center of the strap.

4. Run each end over a kayak and under the bars, then bring the ends together.

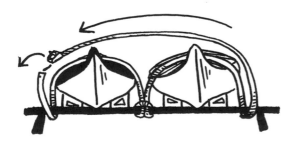

5. The buckle should rest high against a boat so you can tighten the strap by pulling down on the loose end.

6. To adjust the relative lengths of the buckle and loose end, loosen the girth hitch between the kayak and feed the strap in the desired direction.

True Stories

Estimate your strap lengths before you toss the buckle over your boat, or toss the non-buckle end twice.

There's no need to get medieval on your boat when you tie it down.

Run your straps through your stackers to keep the stackers from accidentally folding down.

stacker

It is better to have bow and stern lines and not need them than need them and not have them. Running over the loose end of a bow line can break your boat. To avoid this, some folks tie the bow line to the bumper first. Incidentally, shock cords do not make good bow lines or rack straps.

Park so *your* kayak is on the uphill and upwind side of the stacker.

Creative Transportation

Let he without exhaust cast the first stone. Despite what SUV manufacturers would have you believe, you can kayak without a car.

Progressive Paddling

If possible, store your kayak and gear near the water and bike or ride public transportation instead of driving. For a smog-free full body workout you can carry your boat on your bike with an Extracycle attachment. They are revolutionary!

Airplanes

Call first and see what the length and weight restrictions are for your flight. It may be cheaper to classify your kayak as a surfboard or a windsurfer (since you *can* surf and sail in it). You can also ship your boat ahead of you on air freight.

Taxicabs and Rackless Vehicles

If you don't have a rack, pad the roof of the car with a sleeping pad or towel to keep your boat and the car unscratched. Open the car doors first before you strap the boat down. Carry your straps and duct tape on your person and keep your helmet handy for cab rides in Third World countries.

Buses in Third World Countries

Pad the edges of the bus racks to prevent holes in your hull. Avoid sitting over the wheel well, and make sure your window opens.

From Pavement to Wavement
and Back

Access

Do not take access for granted and change clothes discreetly. Respect private property by politely asking owners for use, and take an extra garbage bag along to pick up trash. Don't be a ramp hog, and keep your boat and gear out of the way of bigger boats that really do need a ramp. Plan launching and landing at high tides if possible to avoid long walks.

At the End of the Day

Keep your gear on if you are close to the car so you won't have to carry it. Sponge out as much water as you can before lifting your boat. If you have a helper, lift your end first so any excess water drains away from you. Load your kayak on the car before changing into dry clothes. Send someone back to the beach for a last sweep for little things like paddles and PFDs. Store your kayak out of the sun with a mesh cockpit cover to discourage critters and mildew (see Special Topics). If you are going to suspend your kayak, sling it underneath the hull instead of hanging it from the end toggles.

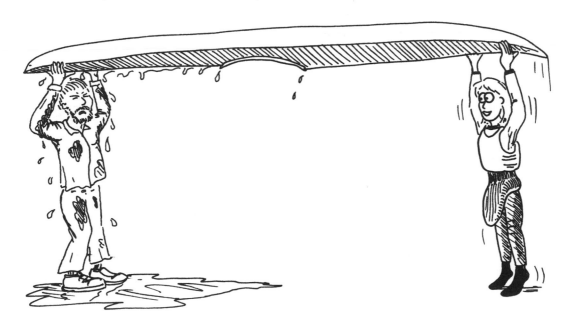

Concepts of Paddling

Eleven Habits of Highly Efficient Paddlers

The following paddling principles are good for beginners to strive for and for experts to revisit. I find I can always improve upon these points.

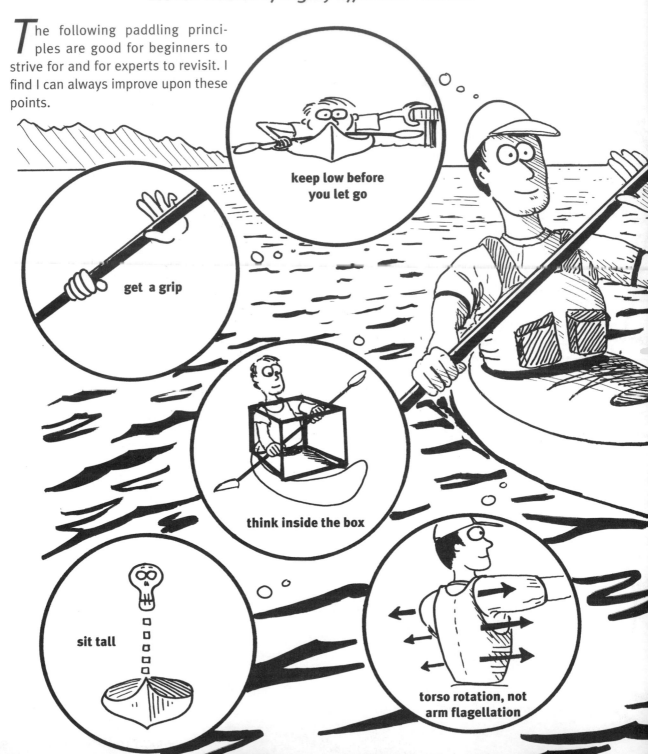

keep low before you let go

get a grip

think inside the box

sit tall

torso rotation, not arm flagellation

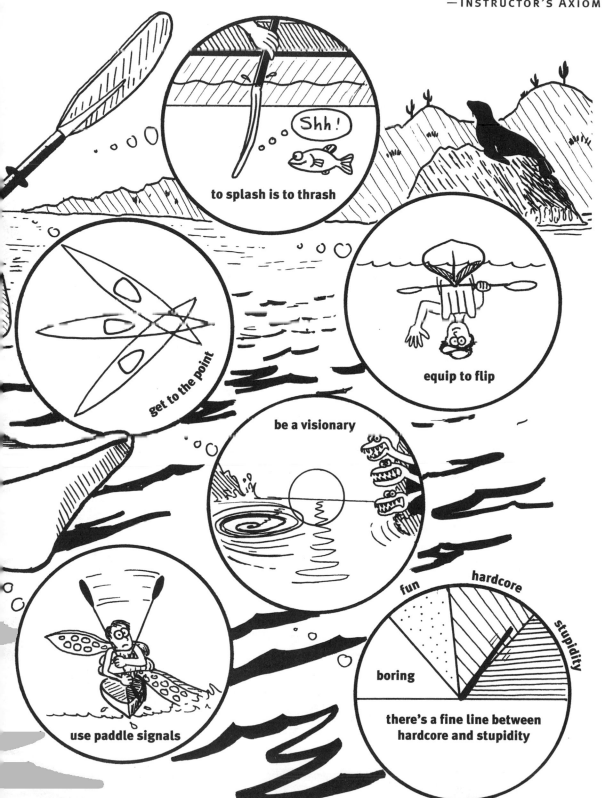

53

Keep Low Before You Let Go

While the put-in and take-out are probably not the most dangerous places to swim, they are the most likely places to swim. The only rule for getting in and out of your kayak is keeping your weight low and centered. The old "put your paddle behind your back" works because it forces you to put your weight on the midline of the kayak, but it thrashes your paddle and isn't always applicable. Learn to get in and out without your paddle by keeping your weight along the midline of the kayak. Have friends stabilize your boat as you get in and out, and remind them to use both hands. Remember to keep your paddle within reach.

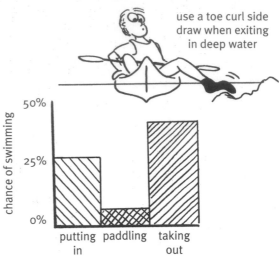

use a toe curl side draw when exiting in deep water

chance of swimming — 50% / 25% / 0%

putting in — paddling — taking out

Dang.

Get a Grip

center

knuckles line up with right blade

left hand nice and loose

apply sunscreen only with left hand

SPF 300

control hand

To find out about where to grip your paddle, place the center of the paddle on your head and grasp the paddle so your upper arms and forearms form a 90° angle. When paddling, keep your right hand fixed on the shaft (this hand is now called the control hand) and let the paddle swivel freely through your left hand. After taking a forward stroke on the right side, lift your right forearm enough to pivot the left blade into position so it catches the water. Avoid tendonitis by holding the paddle loosely with your top hand when paddling for-

ACHOO!

ward. Always try to keep your paddle, wrist, forearm, and elbow lined up in the direction you are pulling the paddle. For certain strokes on your left side, you will have to pivot just your right wrist instead.

straight

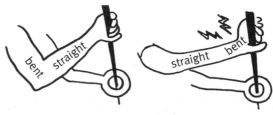

bent — straight — straight — bent

Think Inside the Box!

In order to paddle efficiently and be kinesthetically correct, imagine keeping your hands inside an imaginary box glued to your chest.

To visualize the Paddler's Box, move your paddle from your belly button up to your chin, straight out in front of your face, down to your grab loop, and back to your lap. If you extend your hands outside this box, you rely on wimpy arm muscles instead of strong torso muscles and you expose your shoulder to the possibility of dislocation. It can take a surprisingly small amount of force at the right angle to pop your humerus out of its socket, which is not humerous. This all-too-common injury is usually preventable by proper paddling and rolling technique. If you need to place your paddle at the stern, twist your torso and move your box with you.

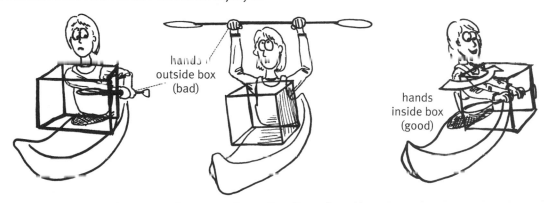

hands outside box (bad)

hands inside box (good)

To Splash Is to Thrash

Splashes and bubbles mean your paddle is acting more like a blender than a flipper. If you want to make miles, not margaritas, move your paddle smoothly and silently through the water. Just because strokes are quiet does not mean that they aren't strong. Stick your paddle in one place like a cross-country ski pole and move your boat past your anchored paddle blade. Make all your strokes better by fully immersing and angling your blade to catch the water throughout all the steps of your stroke.

Sit Tall

Sit up straight! Although kayaking can be relaxing, abandon your Barcalounger or hunchback habits.

Adopt a regal posture to address all your fishy subjects. This posture is the basis for nearly all upright paddling maneuvers. When you sit upright, your paddler's box pivots smoothly from side to side for efficient strokes. In addition, your spine can curve to either side in a C-shaped lean allowing you to tilt your boat over on its side and still stay balanced. Note that when you dip your head to one side your boat tips up to meet it.

small arch in small of back

Your Majesty!

sitting up straight   C-to-C lean

J-lean   bell-buoy lean

As you might suspect, this weird waggle is critical in bracing and rolling. To avoid slouching, try shortening the foot braces to push your hips farther back against the backrest.

The J-lean describes tilting the boat with your lower back while keeping your head and neck straight. The J-lean is often used when bracing into waves or tilting a boat to shorten its waterline. A bell-buoy lean describes a straight spine. If the boat tilts, your center of gravity soon extends beyond your boat's center of buoyancy, and splashdown results.

Leaning forward or backward onto your deck lowers your center of gravity but also limits your ability to lean to the side and twist, essentially freezing you in place at the whim of the waves.

forward and reverse leans freeze your hips

Use Torso Rotation ～ *Not Arm Flagellation*

Torso rotation is the warp drive of kayaking, compared with puny impulse power from your arms. Torso rotation is more than simple shoulder rotation because you twist from your belly button up. When you sit up straight you can twist your upper body and use the large muscle groups in your torso to make paddling easier and more efficient. This motion is the basis for every stroke.

To understand this whole concept of rotation, imagine there is one beer left in the fridge, but it is all the way in the back. If you reach without rotating, the beer is just out of reach. Now twist at your belly so you extend one shoulder forward and the other shoulder backward. In this position not only can you reach the beer, but your whole torso is wound up like a tree branch ready to snap back. As you take the beer out of the fridge (or place your paddle in the water) and untwist, you harness those strong torso muscles and leave your feeble arm-waving friends in your wake. Note that you twist your bottom arm forward and your top arm back at the start of the forward stroke. Once you complete a stroke on one side, you are set up for a stroke on the next side. If you are using proper rotation you should hear a swishing sound from your PFD and paddle jacket on the back deck.

Pivot Points: Get to the Point

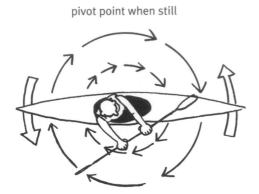

pivot point when still

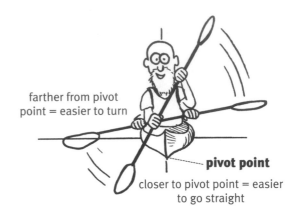

farther from pivot point = easier to turn

pivot point

closer to pivot point = easier to go straight

At some point when you're sea kayaking, you're going to want to turn, and soon after that you're going to want to go straight again. In order to have some control over these matters, you need to know about pivot points.

When you're not making a wake, the pivot point is basically where you're sitting. To go in a straight line without turning, minimize the distance between your blade and your seat. To turn, place your blade farther away and note that your boat turns just as easily from the bow and stern.

As you paddle forward your bow becomes trapped by the bow wave and the pivot point of the boat moves forward. Because the stern is now farthest from the new pivot point, it is usually the most effective place for the rudder and your steering strokes to be. Strokes at the bow and middle of the boat are less effective for steering the boat.

When backpaddling or backsurfing, the pivot point moves toward the stern of the boat and you need to steer from the bow of the boat.

pivot point when moving forward

steering strokes   propulsion strokes

think of your moving kayak like a knife in butter, and apply steering strokes to the free end.

turning strokes

pivot point

Be a Visionary

Beware the Subconscious Magnetic Rock Attraction Effect. We've all witnessed this phenomenon with other sports—skiing, snowboarding, mountain biking, and driving. There's a rock that you really want to avoid, but you just can't stop staring at it. By staring at the obstacle, you are hypnotically drawn straight toward the very thing you want to avoid. The trick is to look where you want to go, and your kayak will magically steer itself on that course.

> Come to me...

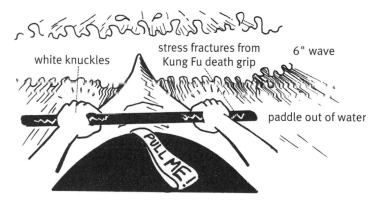

Beginning paddlers focus 6" in front of their bow. Everything is so overwhelming that anything beyond their bow is beyond their capacity to process.

Experienced paddlers know to lift up their gaze to take in the big picture. By being aware of your surroundings, you have more control over your destiny.

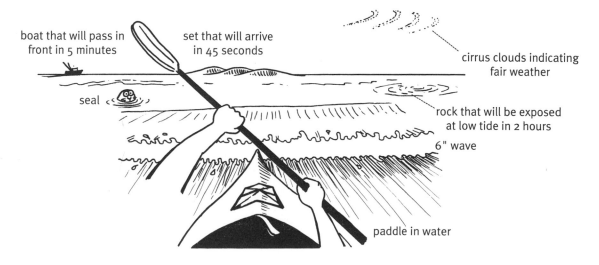

Hydroglyphics or Paddle Signals

Paddle signals are incredibly useful for keeping groups together and communicating basic messages over long distances or over loud surf. Paddle signals are particularly effective for remotely controlling paddlers who would like some guidance landing in the surf zone. Like a game of Simon Says, the person paddling in does exactly what the trustworthy person on the beach signals. Although these examples are given in a surf zone, they can be used any time you're paddling.

Come to Me/Can I Come?

A vertical paddle means "come to me." If given on open water, a group seeing this would gather around the signaler. If given by a paddler on the beach, it means the coast is clear, come on in to shore. Because it is best to land one person at a time in the surf zone, the person waiting outside shore should answer with the same signal to indicate "I'm coming." If you are outside and want clearance to land, you can use this signal to ask if the beach is clear.

Come Quicker!

A vertical paddle vigorously moved up and down means "speed up!" There is probably a big set approaching and your window of opportunity is slamming shut.

Go this Way

A paddle pointing in a particular direction means "go this way" until you receive a different signal. There may be a better landing site in that direction or a deeper channel.

Stop, Hold your Position

A horizontal paddle means "stop and hold your position." This signal is often given because a wave is coming, you are moving out of a good position, or the timing is bad. If you are moving when you receive this signal, use your paddle to stop your momentum lest you coast into the impact zone. This signal can be used to decline a "Can I come?" request.

Go Back!

Paddle blades wagging up and down mean "go back." Stop your forward momentum and start paddling backward. This signal usually means there is a big wave coming and you need to back out of the impact zone pronto.

Are You Okay? Yes, I'm Okay!

Pointing at someone and tapping the top of your head asks them if they are okay. Usually this person has just experienced some mishap and you want to know if they are hurt or not. If someone asks if you are okay and you are okay, respond by tapping on your head.

Danger! Help! I'm Not Okay!

Waving your paddle or arm back and forth is the universal help signal. Use this if you are not okay and are in need of assistance.

Other Signals

no whining

OK but hungry

butthead

you turkey!

Equip to Flip

There are a hundred excuses to avoid practicing rescues, rolls, and recoveries, but if you don't flip over now and then, you're not learning much. Many paddlers experience a plateau in their learning curve after a few seasons.

Steepen your learning curve by throwing yourself into the fray with adequate safety nets in place. The more time you spend upside down the more your comfort level, confidence, self-reliance, and skills will increase. In general, water is pretty soft, so go for it. Usually the worst that will happen is that you swim and have to practice your rescues (have a backup for your backup). When you are practicing, prevent ice cream headaches and make your inversion more enjoyable by wearing the right equipment.

We all have friends who have three boats and all the latest gear, but also have a wide-screen TV and a highspeed Internet connection. While cable television and the Internet have some great paddling information, you're still sitting on your butt on the couch. Remember that surfing is supposed to be an outside activity.

There's a Fine Line between Hardcore and Stupidity

Before trying something sketchy, ask yourself "If I die trying this, will I feel stupid?" Always question your judgment if any of the following factors are involved.

Your Ego
It often is better to wish you had caught a wave than to wish you had not.

Cameras (Kodak Courage Kills)
The sight of a camera brings out the urge to go for the Darwin Award in some people. To complicate matters, photographers are notorious for placing themselves in harm's way for that perfect shot.

Hypothermia
Hypothermia affects your judgment and general ability to cope. Anticipate your clothing needs and energy level and plan accordingly.

Drugs and Alcohol
Much like hypothermia, mind-altering substances impair your judgment.

A New Surf Spot
Get the scoop on a new play spot before getting out there. Ask locals about hazardous rocks, helpful currents, and how these change with the tides.

Boat Obedience

Steering Snafus
- blade too close to pivot point
- paddle not horizontal
- no lean

Kayaks can sense fear. If you are at all nervous, your kayak will turn when you want to go straight and go straight when you want to turn. Instead of taking your disobedient boat back to the dealer, train yourself in kayak communication. Your paddle and body language are your voice, hand signals, leash, collar, and doggie treats combined. This chapter is designed to help you tell your kayak where you want it to go and what you want it to do. Even old kayaks can learn new tricks with this chapter. I also recommend taking a "No Bad Kayaks" class in paddling techniques before any bad habits become ingrained.

Forward Stroke Follies
- all arms
- long curvy strokes
- paddle not vertical

Turning and Steering Strokes

The same steering strokes are used both to turn and to stay on a straight course. Critical components include placing the blade far from the pivot point and tilting your boat to shorten its waterline. If it's not too windy, your turns will be fastest on a wave crest while your bow and stern are out of the water.

The earlier you realize you are off course, the smaller the turning stroke you will need. Beginners wait too long and then overcorrect with exaggerated steering strokes. Observant experts correct any deviations immediately with discrete sweeps and draws.

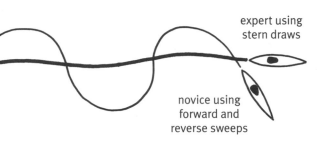

expert using stern draws

novice using forward and reverse sweeps

The Forward Sweep

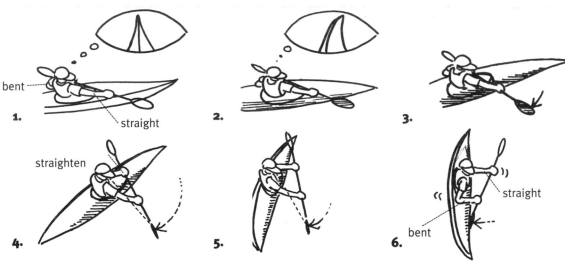

bent
straight

1.
2.
3.

straighten

4.
5.
6.
straight
bent

1. Sit up straight and hold both hands low across your lap. Place your blade past your toes by twisting your torso with your paddle. Extend your reach by straightening your forward arm and bending your rear arm.

2. Submerge your blade and shorten the waterline by tilting your boat toward your paddle. Keep your hands low across your lap.

3. Move your arms and torso as one unit and sweep your blade in a semicircle around your seat. Straighten your rear arm when your blade passes 2:00.

4. Continue to face your paddle blade.

5. Start bending your rear arm when your blade reaches 5:30.

6. Finish with your paddle parallel to the boat and both hands over the water. Drag your rear elbow across the back deck and stretch your front arm out at 3:00.

The Reverse Sweep

The reverse sweep is basically the opposite of the forward sweep.

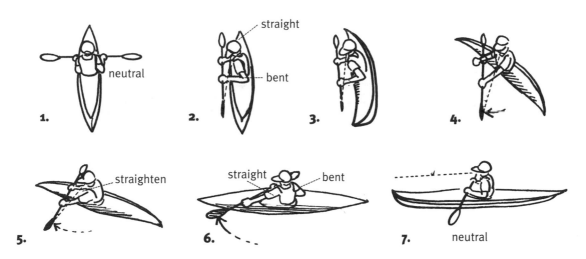

Combining Strokes

When you want to spin quickly from a stationary position, alternate between forward and reverse sweeps on different sides. Pause for a moment and take a breath between strokes to bring your torso back to neutral, then wind your torso up for the next sweep. Remember to tilt the boat toward your working blade. You will find that your strokes eventually blend into one another, with a reverse sweep phasing into a bow draw and then a forward stroke.

Singles vs. Doubles

All these strokes apply to both single and tandem boats, but remember that turning strokes should be as far from the pivot point as possible. For a double kayak at rest, place turning strokes at the bow and stern and skip the parts in the middle which are close to the pivot point. For a cruising double, the steering strokes should be at the stern.

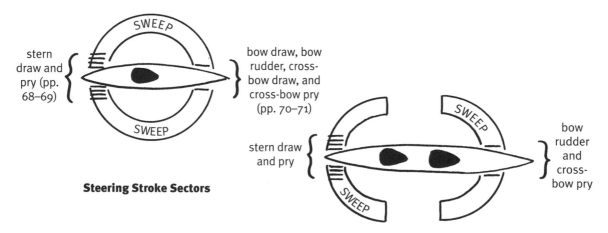

Steering Stroke Sectors

The Stern Draw

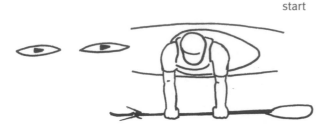

start   finish

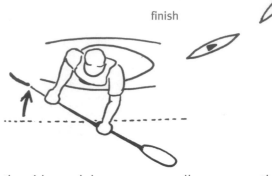

The stern draw is simply the last part of the forward sweep. Use it when you want to turn the bow away from the side your blade is on without losing speed. For course corrections, a forward stroke with a stern draw is more efficient than a forward sweep. Start by twisting your torso to the side and holding the paddle parallel to the boat with both hands held level over the water. Dip your rear blade two feet from the stern deck, push your front hand out directly to the side, and drag your rear elbow across the back deck. Watch your blade to make sure it's submerged, angled to catch water, and far enough behind you. With more practice you won't need to watch it. To start from the end of a forward stroke, slice your blade from your hip away and behind your cockpit to 5:00. An option for more maneuverable shorter boats is to lift your forward arm to chest level at the end of your stroke.

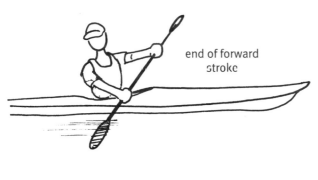

end of forward stroke

slice out to start the stern draw

short boat finish

square

don't be a square!

sea kayak finish

Don't be a square! If you use your bicep correctly, there shouldn't be any daylight between your elbow and body at the end of this stroke!

The Stern Pry or Rudder

Because the stern pry or rudder is one of the most intuitive strokes, it is overused and often misused. Use it when you are surfing or need a quick course correction. The stern pry resembles the start of the reverse sweep except it has no forward component. Start by twisting to the side you want the bow to turn toward and place your paddle parallel to the boat with both hands over the water.

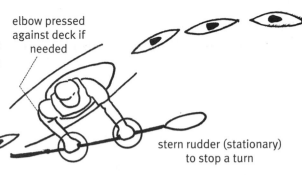

elbow pressed against deck if needed

stern rudder (stationary) to stop a turn

To initiate a turn when going straight, lower your rear hand so the rear blade knifes into the water parallel to the kayak like a rudder. Push your rear hand out away from the boat (not forward) and keep your front hand in place out over the water to act like a fulcrum.

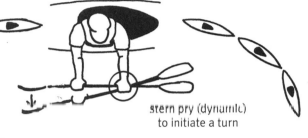

stern pry (dynamic) to initiate a turn

If your boat is already turning in an unintended direction, you can use a static version to turn back on course. Turn your body as before, but instead of placing the paddle parallel with the boat, place your rear blade next to the hull with your front hand over the water. Because your stern is skidding out toward your blade, a stationary rudder is all you need to stop the turn. If your rear arm muscles tire from holding outward pressure, press your rear elbow onto the rear deck and let your skeleton do the work. If you still need to turn more, push your rear hand outward and execute a stern pry.

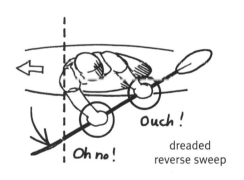

Ouch !

Oh no !

dreaded reverse sweep

The stern pry can easily mutate into a speed-killing reverse sweep if you move your rear hand forward or you bring your front hand in across your lap. If you don't want to lose speed, follow your stern pry with a forward sweep on the opposite side, or use a stern draw instead of a pry.

Hey! Wait for me!

stern pry mutating into a reverse sweep

Bow Draw

Use the bow draw when you are moving slowly forward (or backward) and need a precise turn. Initiate your turn with a sweep and use the bow draw as a pivot point, giving you additional control.

1. Turn your torso as far as you can in the direction you want to turn. 2. Place your blade in the water 45° from the bow with the power face facing the bow. The forearm of your top hand should be next to your forehead as though you were looking at a watch. Your lower arm should be bent with the elbow pressed next to your body.

3. Bring your blade to your knees, then lift it straight up with your forward hand and repeat if needed.

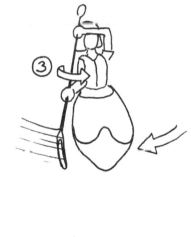

power face

Cross Bow Draw

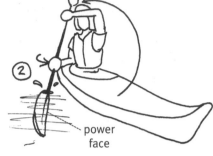

The cross-bow draw accomplishes the same thing as the bow draw but uses stronger muscle groups.

1. Wind up as you would for a forward sweep, but don't stop when your blade is at your bow. Keep twisting until your blade crosses your bow and is well over the water on the other side.

2. When you cannot stretch any farther, lower your forward hand to submerge your blade and keep your rear hand in place.

3. Without moving your arms, use your torso to bring your knees to the blade. When your blade reaches the boat, lift your blade straight out of the water and repeat. You can also bring the paddle back to your usual side and continue with a forward sweep. Remember to start your turn with a sweep stroke, then use these draws to tighten your turn.

Bow Rudder

As the name implies, this stroke is used to steer from the bow when moving backward. This stroke is simply the beginning of the forward sweep frozen just as your blade enters the water at your bow. The stern of your boat will turn toward whichever blade is in the water. Leaning forward slightly will move the paddle farther from the pivot point located behind you. Lifting your top hand digs the paddle blade deeper under the water. If you revert to a normal forward sweep, you will turn more but also lose more speed.

Cross-Bow Pry

Originally an advanced whitewater canoe stroke, the cross-bow pry complements the bow rudder when backsurfing. Instead of steering with alternating bow rudders, try a bow rudder on one side and a cross-bow pry on the other. From a bow rudder, lift your forward blade up and over your bow to the other side of your boat and drop it against the bow. The blade now resembles a streamlined surfboard fin instead of an off-kilter rudder, and it will turn your boat toward the blade. For a stronger stroke, submerge your blade farther by straightening your rear arm so the paddle is almost vertical. The tricky part about backsurfing with this stroke is leaning away from your blade to avoid catching an edge on the face of the wave.

backsurfing with a bow rudder

backsurfing with a cross-bow pry

adjust your blade depth

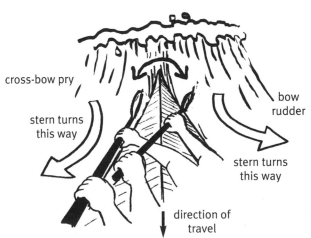

cross-bow pry

stern turns this way

bow rudder

stern turns this way

direction of travel

Help from Your Hips

When you want to turn quickly while moving forward, combine your forward sweep with a lean to the outside of the turn. If you tilt the boat to the right with a J-lean and sweep on the right, most

no lean (ok)

lean to outside of turn (better)

mirror on bottom

kayaks will turn left and vice versa. Paddling faster accentuates this turn. As you lean, your hull shape changes from a symmetrical spear to an angled wing that turns one way more than the other. A hard chine may enhance and control this effect by becoming a curved keel. By leaning away from the turn, your rudder, along with the majority of your hull, skims through the water instead of bulldozing into it.

If you try this counter lean while using your rudder to turn, you may find it hard to both push your foot brace and lift your knee in a counter lean. Consider crossing your rudder cables for better ergonomics.

If you feel a little unbalanced with your forward sweep and outside lean, follow with a skimming low brace (see In the Soup in the Kayak Surfing chapter) on the outside

of the turn instead of a normal forward stroke on the inside of the turn. Reverse sweeps on the inside and hard ruddering may actually delay your turn by slowing down the kayak.

Cool!

Side Strokes

direct route to Peanut M&Ms

beginner's spiral to raisin dregs

You want to get from Point A to Point B before your friends strip-mine all the M&Ms from the gorp. Most beginners take the circuitous route above and land backward ten minutes later when nothing is left except raisins (blegh). An effective side stroke is your best shortcut to the munchies, the dock, a capsized companion, or wherever.

Paddle Position

For an effective side stroke, turn your chest in the direction you want to go and hold your paddle vertically next to your hip. Your hands should be stacked on top of each other with your top hand at face level, as if you could read your watch. Your top forearm should be level and your bottom elbow tucked against your side. Hold the paddle loosely with your top hand and control the blade angle with your bottom hand.

Ready? Turn the page. . . .

Lame side stroke...

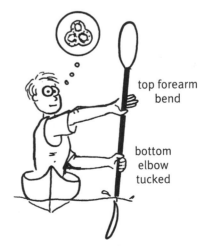

top forearm bend

bottom elbow tucked

Instead, start like this.

The Standard Side Draw

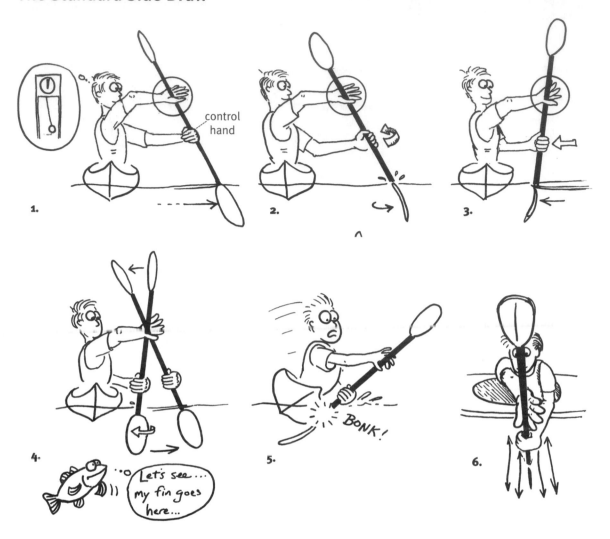

1. Without moving your top hand, slice the blade out by extending your lower hand (knuckles forward). Think of your top hand as the fixed point of a pendulum, while your bottom hand swings the blade out and back. 2. Once you have reached as far out as you can, rotate the paddle shaft 90° so the blade is parallel with your boat and the back of your hand faces the stern. 3. Keep your top hand still and move your bottom hand back toward the boat. Your boat should slip toward your blade. 4. Stop before your blade bumps your boat, feather the blade 90° again (palm in, knuckles forward, back hand out), and slice your blade out again. Repeat as needed. 5. If you don't stop your blade, you will trip over your paddle and fling yourself into the sea. 6. Practice slicing the paddle out by keeping the blade in slice mode (knuckles forward) and swishing the blade out and back repeatedly. When you can slice your paddle in and out twenty times with no mistakes you are ready to turn the paddle into the catch position and draw yourself on over to the side.

The Sculling Side Draw

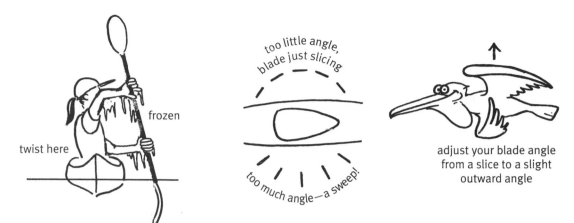

twist here

frozen

too little angle, blade just slicing

too much angle—a sweep!

adjust your blade angle from a slice to a slight outward angle

This sensual, sleek, and subtle version of the side draw is much easier for some people. Glue your bottom elbow to your side and your top forearm to your forehead and pivot at your waist.

Just like a sweep stroke, the sculling side draw describes an arc around the cockpit except that your paddle shaft is vertical and the blade is close to your hip. Instead of catching the water to turn the boat, open your blade to slightly swish through the water so your boat scoots toward your paddle. Imagine yourself smearing creamy peanut butter along the side of your boat with your blade. Once you reach one end of the arc, reverse directions and adjust the blade angle to climb away from the kayak again. If one end of your boat waggles more than the other and gets ahead, concentrate your sculling closer to the end lagging behind until it catches up.

PEANUT BUTTER

The Side Slip

This maneuver can be handy when you spot that submerged rock five feet in front of your bow. Turn to the side you want to slip toward and plant your blade in a sculling draw position just in front of your hip. Adjust the blade placement and angle as needed to keep your kayak sliding over evenly. If your boat turns toward your paddle instead of side slipping, you have just done a bow draw (cool, but not as cool as a side slip). Transform this bow draw into a side slip by placing your last forward stroke on the same side you want to side slip toward to cancel the turn. Look for an asymmetrical bow wake to see if you are really side slipping.

awesome asymmetrical bow wake

Boat Lean

Sea kayaks with V-shaped hulls may side slip most easily if you tilt the boat toward the paddle, allowing the water to slip past the boat's keel, but be careful of leaning too far. Boats with hard chines or flat-bottomed planing hulls side slip best if you tilt the boat away from the paddle so the sharp chine doesn't catch.

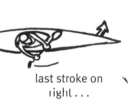

last stroke on left . . .

. . . right turn

last stroke on right . . .

. . . right side slip

V-hull—
tilt toward paddle

planing-hull—
tilt away from paddle

Propulsion Strokes

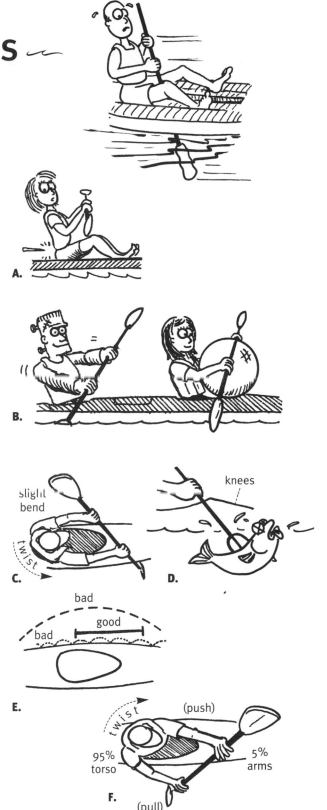

Ideally, propulsion strokes would run down the middle of the boat, but since this is not a viable option, try the next best thing by keeping your paddle shaft as vertical as you can and your strokes short.

The Forward Stroke

The more you know about paddling, the more you realize you need to work on your forward stroke. The efficiency of your stroke is magnified tremendously over five miles or five days, so it pays to be mindful of your mechanics.

A. This is a reminder to sit up straight in case you're slouching again.

B. Keep your paddle at arm's distance away by imitating Frankenstein's monster or imagining that there is a huge beach ball between you and your paddle. This technique forces you to move your arms and torso as one unit.

C. Just like winding up for a golf stroke or baseball swing, wind your body up for your forward stroke. When you can't twist anymore, it is time for the next step.

D. Without leaning forward, stab your paddle blade in the water as if you were spearing a fish. This visualization helps your blade grip the water during the most important part of the stroke. Most of your power comes during the first 6" when your torso is first unwinding.

E. Without scraping your hull, keep your stroke close to and parallel with the keel of the boat.

F. Twist instead of push and pull. Your torso and arms should move as one unit. Some independent arm movement is fine, but it should be subsidiary to your torso motion.

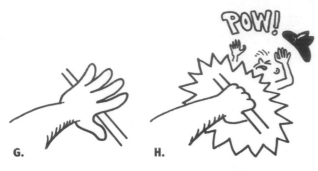

G.　**H.**

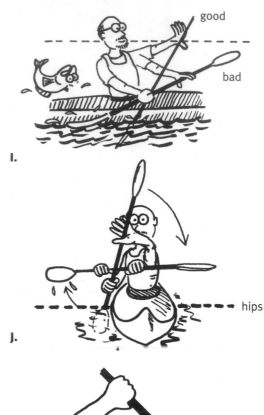

good

bad

hips

I.

J.

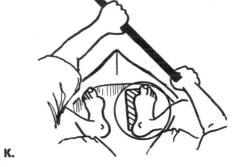

K.

G. Relax your wrist and push your paddle with the open palm of your top hand.

H. Punch this hand forward like you're knocking out a bad guy. Keep your upper hand at chin level throughout your stroke.

I. If you drop your top hand down, your blade simply splashes up out of the water.

J. Keep your stroke short and slice your blade out at your hip. Your torso will then be set up for a forward stroke on your other side. Long, lingering strokes just lift water up or turn the kayak instead of propelling the boat forward.

K. Step on the gas. Translate your stroke to your boat by pushing forward with the foot on the same side you're paddling on.

L. To avoid becoming tangled in kelp or milfoil, leave your blade in the water at the end of the stroke while you glide forward. Your blade will drift behind you and the slime will slide off. This pause is similar to gliding while cross-country skiing.

Kelp!

L.

The Scoot Stroke

M. Use an aggressive rocking motion when stranded on rocks or sandbars.

M.

The Reverse Stroke

Lobsterboats, swimmers, seals, and other kayakers will all appreciate your ability to put on the brakes. If you stop paddling forward you will not automatically stop. A good reverse stroke is the best way to stop as well as back up. Backing up in a straight line is a good way to enter sea caves because you can keep an eye on waves. (Be sure to lift your rudder out of the water in these situations.)

Don't change your grip on the paddle to use the concave power face. The convex back face will work just fine.

A. To start, twist to the side and look back behind you, and place your paddle parallel with the boat. B. Dip both knuckles in the water and watch your rear blade. C. Dip your lower hand through the water as you push the blade forward to keep your blade parallel with the keel. Hold your top hand over the water to keep your paddle shaft vertical. D. Slice your paddle out at your knees. E. Look over your other shoulder to wind up for the next stroke. F. To steer, use the tail end of a reverse sweep, a bow draw, a cross-bow draw, or a bow rudder instead of your boat's rudder.

A.

B.

C.

D.

E.

F.

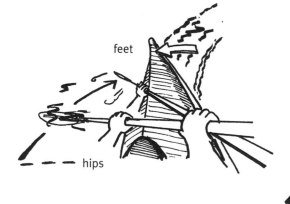

feet

hips

Rescues

"Just sit right back and you'll hear the tale, the tale of a fateful trip."
—Theme from "Gilligan's Island"

There are two kinds of kayakers: Those that have flipped and those that are going to flip. But now what do you do? Regardless of whether you are going to punch out of your boat before your hair gets wet, or hand roll back up, this chapter applies to you.

Reading about these methods is not going to do you any good if you don't practice them in realistic conditions (not just a swimming pool). So after practicing them in the warmth of a swimming pool or in a warm lake, grab your wetsuit and flail with a couple of friends in some safe spot when a

hefty wind is blowing onshore. Learn what works for you and have backup plans for your backup plan. Decks and cockpits cluttered with gear inhibit rescues, so pack wisely and securely.

Surviving Flips ~ (So You Can Be Rescued)

Here are some things to keep in mind so you will be involved in a rescue and not a recovery.

The Tuck

You flipped over! Congratulations! If you don't flip over now and then, you're not trying hard enough. When you flip over, protect your head, shoulders, and other vital organs by leaning forward and pressing your nose against the front of your cockpit. In this position you are set up for an Eskimo roll, an Eskimo rescue, AND a wet exit. If you don't assume this position, gravity will pull your body toward the bottom where the rocks and sea slugs live.

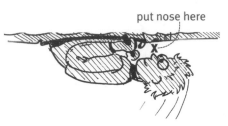

put nose here

A common beginner reaction is to arch the back onto the back deck of the kayak. In this position a beginner is perfectly set up for nasal dredging of the bottom.

ESKIMO ROLL, page 87

ESKIMO BOW RESCUE, page 98

WET EXIT, page 83

Smooch!

no tuck

grab loop

I'm FINE, thanks.

The Wet Exit

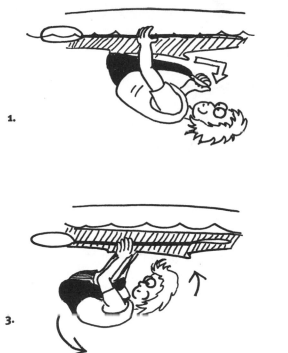

A wet exit turns a seaworthy unit of kayak and kayaker into a tub full of water and a maladapted mammal in need of a rescue. Reserve wet exits for situations when there are no other options to breathe. A wet exit is not a rescue but cause for a rescue. Knowing how to wet exit does not mean you know how to rescue yourself. It should be practiced, perfected, and avoided. Swimming inconveniences and possibly endangers you and the other paddlers in your group. Learn to roll. Your friends will appreciate it.

What do you do with your paddle while rescuing others or being rescued? If you are in the water and need to use your hands, tuck your paddle under an arm or hold it between your legs. If you are in your boat, tuck the paddles between your elbows and your belly.

1. While tucked, let go of the paddle with one hand and pop your sprayskirt. 2. While staying in your tuck, place your hands on your boat by your hips and take the kayak off just like a pair of pants. 3. Once your butt is out, bring your legs out. Do not twist to the side, as your legs or feet may become caught inside. 4. Roll forward in an underwater somersault and head for the surface, always holding onto the kayak and paddle.

A Fool and His Boat Are Soon Parted

Your kayaker-less kayak can sail out of your reach in a second if you let go. A leg inside the cockpit will keep you with your boat and free your hands. If you lose a boat, one person should stay with the swimmer while another retrieves or detains the kayak. If you are the only rescuer, you have to choose between towing the swimmer to the boat or the boat to the swimmer. If the swimmer is perfectly safe, you can opt for the boat, but you may not have time to empty the water before

towing it back. Towing the swimmer may be the best option in cold water. You can have the swimmer scramble onto your stern like a surfboard provided you can handle a hitchhiker.

Emptying the Water

The more flotation you have, the less water you will have to empty. Keep your boat upside down until you have a drain plan. If you have a bulkhead behind your seat, lift up the bow of the overturned boat to drain the water. Break the suction by rolling the edge of the cockpit to the surface.

If there are no bulkheads, teeter-totter the kayak in the shallows or across a kayak. If you can't prop an end but can still stand up, try the flip and drip. 1. Press down your end of the righted kayak so the water rushes toward you. 2. Lift your end up and quickly flip the kayak upside down. 3. Flip the boat back upright and repeat.

If you are sitting in a boat full of water, friends can help pump the water out or you can climb on someone's bow while they seesaw the water out across their boat. If the seas are rough, put your skirt on and pump from a gap on the down-wave side.

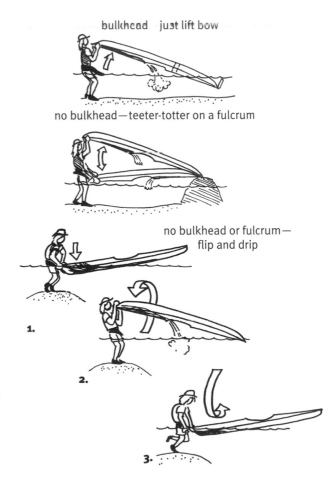

bulkhead   just lift bow

no bulkhead—teeter-totter on a fulcrum

no bulkhead or fulcrum—
flip and drip

1.

2.

3.

Self-Rescues ～

Hip Snaps and Head Dinks for the Hesitant

Avoid wet exits by using the hip snap and head dink, crucial components to braces, Eskimo rescues, and Eskimo rolls. This motion involves scrunching one side of your head, ribs, hips, knees, and toes together. To dink your head, face forward and drop your ear to the side (turning your head and looking to the side is not a dink).

Common sense tells you to lift your head up when submerged in a hostile aqueous environment. Unfortunately, this is precisely the wrong thing to do if you are off-balance in a kayak. The muscles that lift your head also, by an equal and opposite reaction, roll your kayak farther over. The muscles that dink your head help right your boat.

Practice your hip snap by making waves with your hull. Next, find a bow, pool side, or low dock, lay both hands on one side, and rest your ear on your hands. Tilt the kayak over toward your hands by lifting your knee on the side away from your hands. To right your kayak, press the side of your head down on your hands, lift the knee closest to your hands, and press harder on your foot pedals to transfer this motion to your kayak. Keep your ear on your hands longer than you think you have to, as lifting your head too soon kills your hip snap. Practice this motion on both sides and try a little head dink the next time you find yourself straying off the vertical plane.

Braces

The brace is a preemptive self-rescue consisting of a head dink with a little paddle support. Be certain to keep your elbows close to your side when bracing to protect your shoulders against dislocation. Sitting up straight is crucial for the hip snap/head dink. I prefer high braces on high

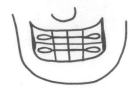

foam piles and low braces on low foam piles or in very shallow water.

High Brace

The high brace is performed with knuckles up, the paddle power face down, and elbows low and tight into your side. As you tip toward one side, slap the paddle power face down, dink your head down to that side, and lift up your

lower knee in a hip snap. Recover by keeping your head to the side, tilting your boat up away from your brace, and centering your paddle across your chest.

Low Brace

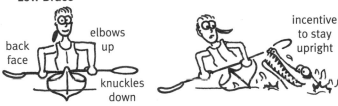

The low brace is performed with the power face up, knuckles down, and the elbows positioned directly above your wrists. As you slap the back

face of the paddle down, hip snap and head dink. Recover by rolling your knuckles forward.

Common Mistakes

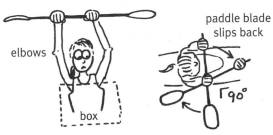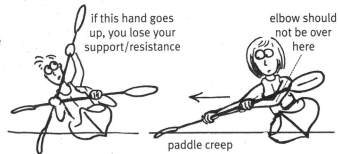

Common problems include elbows above the paddler's box, the blade not at 90° to the boat, the one-handed paddle lift, and paddle creep

out away from the boat. Remember that if your brace fails, immediately tuck forward to protect your noggin!

Rolling Your Kayak

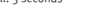

Roll: 3 seconds   vs.

Why Roll?

Rolling is far safer than swimming and saves vast amounts of you and your group's time and energy. Learn from someone who knows how to teach a roll, not just someone who knows how to roll. You have to be committed to learning, practicing, and using your roll if you want it to be there for you. The C-to-C and sweep rolls described here are two of many rolls and form the foundation of other rolls.

No roll: one minute to never

Roll Reminders

Wear a helmet, earplugs, and noseplugs to keep your head happy. Set up by leaning forward, tucking your head, and placing your paddle on the side of the boat. Crunch up toward one knee so your knuckles are out of the water and your forward paddle blade is flat on the surface. Protect your shoulders by keeping your elbows low and close. You can salvage a less-than-perfect roll with a strong finish position.

Rolling on Both Sides

All it takes is one time trying to roll up against a wave to realize the necessity of having a roll on both sides. Learn in a warm pool with a good instructor and practice by rolling only on your off-side for the next month. Adopt the habit of switching sides if you miss a roll. Soon you won't have a preference for which side you roll on.

"I'm in a nice warm pool."

The C-to-C Roll

The C-to-C roll is named because of the shape your spine makes at the crux and finish of the roll. This roll is particularly easy for kayakers who are flexible and long armed.

1st C   2nd C

1. setup from bow

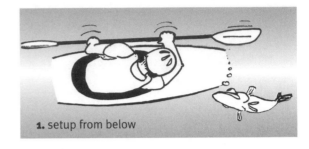

1. setup from below

2. sweep

sore on thumb from good technique

both hands out of water

head stretched to surface

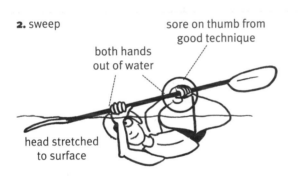

2. sweep from below

From your setup (1), wrap your rear arm around the hull of the boat so your rear hand is resting on the hull by your butt. Sweep your front hand and head out to 90°, crunching your abdomen and side muscles so your ear and hands are out of the water and in a C shape (2).

Once your body is extended in this position, immediately dink your head and snap your hips to make a "C" on the opposite side. At the same time, pull your extended hand down across your face to rest at your chest (3). Your other hand acts as the pivot point for your roll, so do not move that elbow. Your body will roll up and meet this elbow at your side.

Finish this roll facing forward with your head tilted to the side, your paddle centered above your belly button, both elbows tucked in, and your boat tilted slightly (4).

3. hip snap and head dink

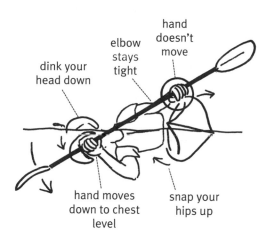

dink your head down

elbow stays tight

hand doesn't move

hand moves down to chest level

snap your hips up

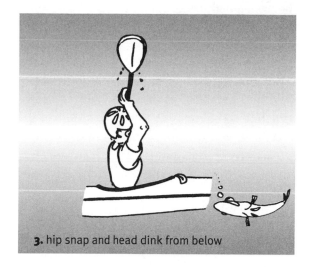

3. hip snap and head dink from below

4. breathe!

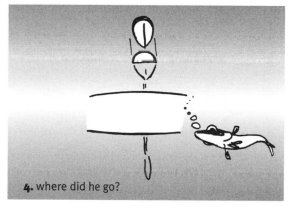

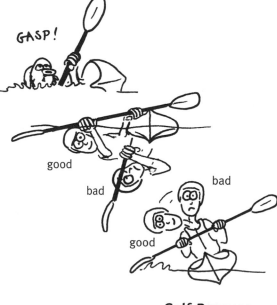

4. where did he go?

We've all performed this magic trick: the disappearing roll; here yesterday and gone today. Rolls turn into flails if you are tired or forget about these key points:

• Take time to set up and stretch your head to the surface before you snap.

• When you hip snap, drop your ear onto your shoulder and keep it there.

• Don't lift your upper hand or you will lose your support.

bad

good

GASP!

good

bad

bad

good

The Sweep Roll

The sweep roll is a good choice for kayakers who do not consider themselves very flexible, and is a reliable roll in general. Some people do a C-to-C roll on one side and a sweep roll on the other. Instead of using a head dink and side crunch to right the boat, you twist your shoulders to one side and your hips move to the

other side, righting the boat. The hand farthest from the blade actually controls the blade angle. As you sweep, lift your forearm from your lap to your chin.

setup

knuckles up

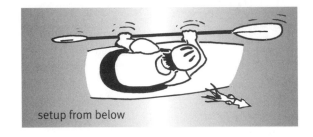

setup from below

1. start sweep

watch your paddle blade

start hip snap here

no hip snap yet

1. from below

2.

knuckles and forearm roll back

2. from below

1. From the setup, sweep your front hand out so your front blade skims across the surface about two feet from your hull.

2. Continue slicing your blade across the surface and start lifting your opposite knee with a hip snap as you turn your shoulders. Turn your head and shoulders to watch the blade.

3.

4.

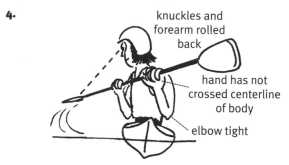

knuckles and
forearm rolled
back

hand has not
crossed centerline
of body

elbow tight

3. from below

3. Your hip snap should be complete as your paddle sweeps past 90°. Keep watching your blade.

4. The finish position consists of your body sitting upright (not leaning back), twisted to face your blade. Make sure your far hand is below your chin and has not crossed the centerline of your body.

Problem Solving Your Sweep Roll

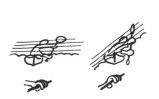

1. If you find yourself stalled on your side, wiggle your hips so you flip completely upside down.

Where am I?

2. Don't start your hip snap until your blade is a foot or two from your bow.

3. Watch your paddle blade throughout your sweep.

good   bad

4. Raise the forearm of your rear hand from your lap to your chin (this keeps your blade angle the same as you roll up).

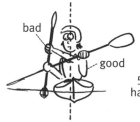

bad

good

5. Do not bring your upper hand across the centerline of your body.

bad

6. To protect your shoulders and be ready to paddle, twist back instead of leaning back.

Other Self-Rescue Options

(When Good Rolls Go Bad)

In case you flip over and your roll disappears (or has never quite appeared), you will need a system to get you from a wet exit back into your kayak. All these backup systems take longer, require more gear, and are colder than a roll, but they are better than The Big Swim back to shore (which may not be an option). Just like the roll, you need to practice these if you want to be able to use them.

The Scramble Rescue

Simply crawl on your deck and slide back in your seat. Needless to say, agility, speediness, and calm conditions all help. Sit-on-top paddlers excel at this rescue. To go for a swim without tipping over, do the scramble rescue in reverse.

1. After you right your kayak by pushing up on the nearest side, hold onto the stern deck and bring your heels to the surface behind you.

2. Slide your stomach onto your deck. You can skip a step from here by rolling over so your butt lands in the cockpit. If you don't have a rudder, you can crawl up the stern with your sprayskirt grab loop in your teeth to avoid snagging it.

3. Crawl forward until your hips are over the cockpit and you are lying on your kayak like a surfboard.

4. Sit up in a straddle and drop your butt into the cockpit so your legs hang over the sides in a surprisingly stable position.

5. Bring your legs in, pulling back your shins with your hands if needed, and start pumping.

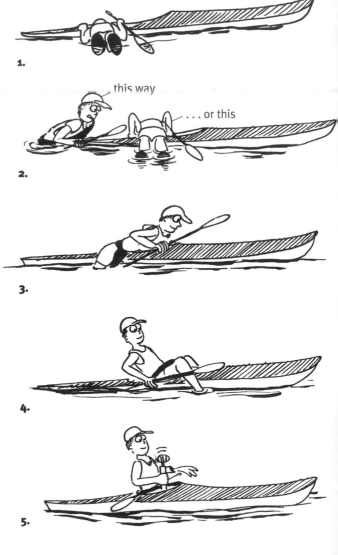

The Re-Enter and Roll with a Paddle Float

This Harry Houdini-esque rescue involves reseating yourself in your inverted kayak and performing a head dink off your paddle float. Although it sounds daunting, this is the easiest self-rescue option in stormy seas next to a roll. If you have a strong roll, you can skip the paddle float part.

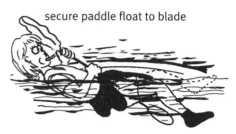

secure paddle float to blade

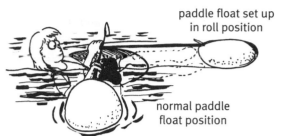

paddle float set up in roll position

normal paddle float position

1. Float on your back on the windward side of the boat, facing the bow, and hook your foot in the cockpit to stay with your boat. Retrieve your paddle float from its easy-access storage place, attach it securely to your paddle, and inflate it fully.

2. Place the paddle across the hull at 90° to your kayak and hold it there with the hand closest to the boat. If you are familiar with rolling, you can also place it parallel with the boat with the paddle float toward the bow.

3. With your free far hand, reach underwater to the far side of the cockpit (you will have to dunk your head in the process).

4. Pull your knees, hips, and feet back in place. Once you are seated securely, grab the paddle with both hands.

5. If your paddle is parallel to the boat, sweep it out to 90°. Just like a brace, dink your head down and roll your boat upright with your knees.

6. Keep your weight over your paddle float as you pump the water out.

Paddle Float Rescue

This rescue is a combination of Twister and The Limbo because you use a paddle float to climb and pivot back into the boat while keeping your center of gravity as low as possible on the paddle float side of the kayak.

Just as with the re-enter and roll, float on your back on the windward side of the boat with your leg inside the cockpit to stay with your boat. Hold your paddle while you find your paddle float from its easy-access storage place, secure it over the blade, and inflate it. Grab your boat, remove your leg, and flip your kayak right side up by pushing the cockpit up and away from you. Make sure you have a good grip on the opposite side of the coam-

ing so the kayak doesn't blow away.

1. Move aft of the cockpit and grab your paddle shaft and cockpit coaming in your foremost hand with your paddle float beside you. Grab a stern deck line with the other hand. If you have short legs you can do this maneuver in front of the paddle, next to the cockpit.

2. Float your feet up to the surface behind you, and use both hands to slide your stomach onto your deck. Keep pressure on the paddle float!

3. Flop your forward foot over the paddle for a third point of contact.

4. Flop your other foot over the paddle.

1.

2.

3.

4.

5. keep your weight over the paddle float

6.

7. stay low

9. right hand   left hand

switch grips carefully— one hand at a time

5. Pivot on your belly to swing your forward foot into the cockpit.

6. Reach underneath the leg on the paddle with your aft hand and grab the paddle shaft. Keep hold of the paddle shaft and rear cockpit coaming with your other hand.

7. Now move your other leg into the cockpit so you are belly down on your kayak holding the paddle with both hands.

8. Turn toward the paddle float and slide your butt into the cockpit. Keep pressure on the paddle float!

9. Change your grip as you go so the paddle ends up behind you.

10. Move the paddle in front of you and keep your weight over it as you pump the water out and fit your sprayskirt back on. Another option is to fasten your paddle like an outrigger if your kayak is so equipped, freeing both hands for pumping.

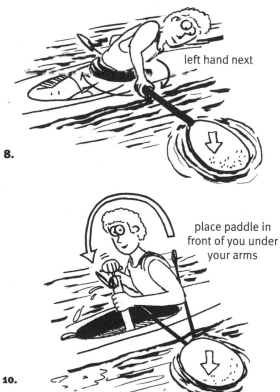

8. left hand next

10. place paddle in front of you under your arms

Assisted Rescues

Even if you never miss your roll, at some point one of your friends will and it would be best to know what to do. Being comfortable with these rescues will turn most swims from escalating emergencies into fun campfire stories.

The AMF YO YO Principle

Before you rush in to rescue others, make sure that you don't end up needing a rescue as well and create a fuster cluck. Jumping out of your boat rarely helps anyone and simply complicates the situation. In these instances, invoke the AMF Yo Yo Principle (Adios my friend, you're on your own). You can still help your friends from a safe distance by giving directions, providing moral support, or signaling for outside help.

Raft Up and Rest—the Pre-Rescue!

Rescues are easier and less likely to be needed if your group stays together. Rafting up and checking in with each other gives people a chance to deal with hypothermia, dehydration, hunger, and haplessness while everyone is still in their boats. If you are paddling outside your comfort zone, let someone know before you need a rescue. If paddlers keep falling behind, let them rest before heading off again. Consider having a stronger paddler tow the straggler (see towing at the end of this chapter). When rafting up, pick a safe location well outside the surf zone and make sure your fingers don't get crunched between boats.

The Hand of God Rescue

This rescue is popular with whitewater instructors but is also possible with longer boats if the capsized kayaker remains composed. Paddle alongside the overturned boat and place your paddle between the boats or under your arms. Grab the outside edge of the overturned boat with your far hand and press down with your other hand to push and pull the boat upright. If the person is unable to tuck forward as they should, guide the person's body into a layback position as with a Scoop Rescue (see below). This maneuver is surprisingly easy if the other person knows to remain tucked, but difficult if he or she does not. This is also a good rescue when the rescuer is wading in water, a common roll-teaching scenario (wear a helmet to keep from getting bonked with a paddle).

Scoop Rescue

The scoop is an extension of a Hand of God rescue for an incapacitated swimmer.

Approach with the swimmer's boat between you and the swimmer, bow to stern if possible. Tilt the boat over so the cockpit is low enough to slide the swimmer into. Reach across, grab the swimmer, and guide his legs and hips all the way into the cockpit. As with the re-enter and roll, it is important for the swimmer to be fully seated. Grab his PFD, lean him back to the rear deck, and pull him upright.

The Eskimo Bow Rescue for Hydrophobics

"It's not the flip, it's the recovery that counts."
— KARLA VANDER ZANDEN, CANYONLANDS FIELD INSTITUTE

In an Eskimo Bow Rescue, a capsized kayaker uses another kayaker's bow or paddle to right him- or herself. Although longer kayaks may be difficult to maneuver into position in time to prevent a wet exit, these rescues are great if you are following someone closely, have a shorter boat, or want to spot someone's roll. Practice this Eskimo Bow Rescue with the rescue kayak already pointed at the cockpit of the capsizing kayak.

Easing Yourself Over

1. Start with hip snaps off your friend's boat until you are comfortable on both sides. Next, tilt your boat over toward your partner's bow and let go with your farthest hand.

2. Place this hand underwater on the side of your boat and lower yourself with your remaining hand until you are upside down in the water.

3. Once you have reassured yourself that you can get back upright from this position, let go with both hands. Hold onto your paddle in one hand or keep it between your arm and your boat.

Asking For Help

4. Stay tucked and get your friend's attention by tapping, slapping, or pounding on the bottom of your boat. Actively search for her bow by reaching up above the water and moving your hands back and forth between your hips and ankles. Keep your hands a thumb's distance away from your hull so you can move your hand aside before it is crushed by a rescuer's bow.

5. When you feel your friend's bow, grab it and push it forward toward your knees. Place one hand on top of the other and rest your head on your hands.

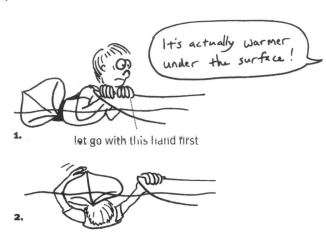

It's actually warmer under the surface!

1. let go with this hand first

2.

gap between fingers and boat

3.

reach back and forth while tucked

4.

5.

push bow to your knees so your fingers face forward

Uh oh. If you grab your friend's bow behind your head, your fingers will be pointed toward your stern (ouch), exposing your shoulders and interfering with your ability to hip snap. If this happens, go back underwater and push the bow forward toward your knees (ahh).

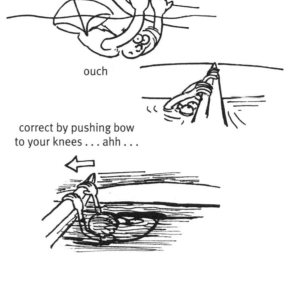

uh oh—bow behind your head

ouch

correct by pushing bow to your knees . . . ahh . . .

Righting Your Boat

6. Now proceed to snap your head into your hands, bring up your lower knee with a hip snap, and rest your head on your hands until your partner says it's OK.

You will notice a dramatic difference between hip snapping back up and lifting with your arms. Try both just so you know never to lift with your arms.

6.

Eskimo Side Rescue with a Paddle

If you are parallel with someone who flips over, you can use your paddle instead of your bow as a rescue platform.

Place your paddle across both your deck and the overturned hull. Reach down to the up-side-down paddler's searching hand, grab his wrist, and place his hand on your paddle shaft. He should be able to do a hip snap off your paddle, coming up slowly to avoid head-banging your hull.

The T-Rescue

This is an adaptation of the Side Rescue that also empties the water by positioning the boats in a T shape. This is the best assisted rescue for most conditions.

bow

1. As the rescuer, grab the inverted bow with both hands, tucking your paddle under your elbows. To stabilize yourself, place your near hand on top of the bow and your far hand underneath it. Have the swimmer hold onto his or her paddle or give it to you for safekeeping. The swimmer can either rest on your bow or hold onto the stern of his boat.

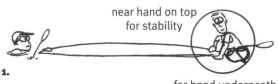

near hand on top for stability

far hand underneath for leverage

2. Tilt your coaming far enough over so it slips under the inverted bow, then tilt your coaming back to lift the other boat's bow out of the water. The swimmer can help by pressing down the stern of the overturned boat.

3. Use both hands to pull the boat across your deck so the water drains out. If there is no rear bulkhead, pull the overturned kayak farther onto your deck and seesaw the water out.

use your cockpit to lever the bow up

seesaw kayaks without bulkheads

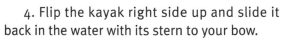

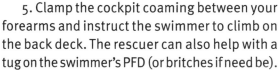

4. Flip the kayak right side up and slide it back in the water with its stern to your bow.

5. Clamp the cockpit coaming between your forearms and instruct the swimmer to climb on the back deck. The rescuer can also help with a tug on the swimmer's PFD (or britches if need be).

bow to stern

feet up on surface

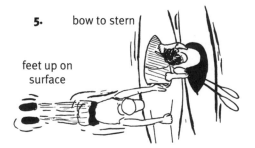
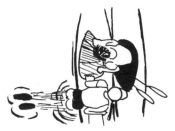

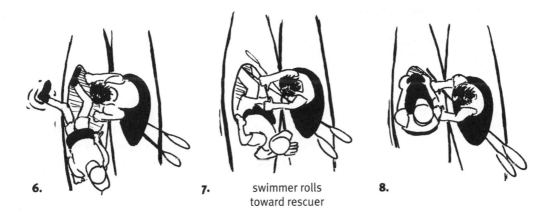

6.   **7.**   swimmer rolls
toward rescuer   **8.**

6. While keeping a low profile and hugging the stern, the swimmer should pivot his toes into the cockpit.

   7. The swimmer should roll toward the rescuing boat and slip his feet and butt back in the boat.

8. As with any assisted rescue, let go of the boat only when the swimmer is both physically and mentally ready to be on his own.

The Side Rescue Variation or "Dump and Pump"

We'd like a side rescue, please!

The Side Rescue is an abbreviated T-rescue that skips the step of emptying the water from the capsized boat. This is the quickest way to get swimmers back into their boats, but they will need some additional stability while they pump the water out. This method is the best place to start with a loaded double. Flip the boat upright quickly so that you scoop up as little water as possible. If you need to vacate the area immediately, you may have to paddle a short way with a boat full of water or use a towing assist. Do not let go of the rescued boat until it is pumped dry and the paddlers have their sprayskirts back on and feel stable.

Slings of Outrageous Fortune

A sling or 12' length of floating line tied in a loop can serve as a stepladder to help paddlers without Spiderman abilities climb up out of the water and back into their kayaks during a paddle float, T, or side rescue. Attach a paddle float on the swimmer's side for solo rescues or when additional support is needed for assisted rescues.

Of the several ways to secure a sling, here are my favorites:

1. For both solo and assisted rescues, slip the swimmer's paddle through the loop, lay the paddle across the boat just behind the cockpit, and hang the sling opposite the swimmer.

2. The swimmer reaches under the boat, retrieves the end of the loop, and brings it up and over the paddle shaft on his side.

3. The swimmer needs to wrap the sling across itself to keep it from slipping and adjust

the length so it reaches a foot below the surface so the swimmer's shin will press against the kayak.

4. Just as with the T-rescue, the swimmer positions himself aft of the paddle, places his foremost foot in the loop, and stands up in the sling as he pulls himself up. A tug on the swimmer's PFD from a rescuer can also help.

5. Once the swimmer is on the back deck of his boat, he needs to carefully remove the sling from his foot before pivoting and sliding back into his seat.

6. A paddle-less option for assisted rescues is to fit the sling around the cockpit of the swimmer's boat so that a section is loose enough to serve as a step. The rescuer can shorten the sling length by tying an overhand knot.

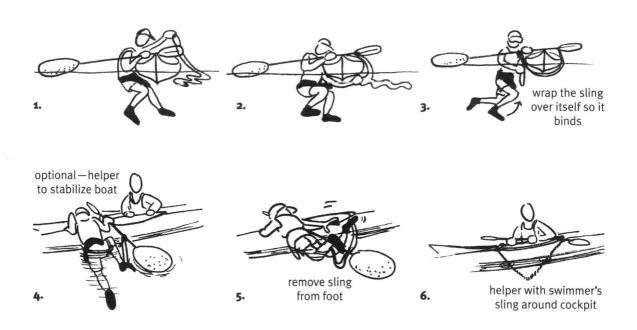

1.

2.

3. wrap the sling over itself so it binds

optional—helper to stabilize boat

4.

5. remove sling from foot

6. helper with swimmer's sling around cockpit

Double Trouble

Side rescues, scrambles, paddle floats, and slings all work well for double kayaks. For a loaded double, avoid rescues involving much lifting or levering, such as the T-rescue. The person with the thickest wetsuit or weakest brace should stabilize the boat by grabbing the cockpit coaming while the other person climbs in. The first person back in the boat then steadies the boat with a paddle float or brace for the second person. Enlist as much help as you can to pump and bail the boat.

Rescuing Swimmers
Swimmer Psychology

Think of your kayak as the Nautilus and a panicky swimmer as a giant squid. Before letting swimmers latch onto your kayak, make sure they are going to follow directions. If they start misbehaving, back off and talk to them until they calm down. If you don't already know, find out if anyone else is out there with them.

Ask for and use their names. In addition to reassuring them, calling them by name helps direct their actions in an emergency. Talking through your rescue plan with them serves to calm them down and remind yourself of your next step: "I'm going to slide your boat across mine and I'll need you to push your stern down." Reassure them throughout the rescue: "We're going to get you back in your boat right away. Nice PFD. Where did you get it?"

Towing Swimmers

To transport someone short distances, have the swimmer hold onto your rear grab loop and kick while you paddle. A more efficient option is for the swimmer to climb up and lie on your stern like a surfboard and hold onto the rear cockpit coaming. Have an apprehensive swimmer hold onto your bow with his or her legs wrapped around the deck like a sloth so you can keep an eye on him.

Tow, Tow, Tow Your Boat

A tow can serve as a jump start for a tired paddler, a winch to get someone away from a dangerous area, or a wrecker for a disabled kayaker or kayak. Giving a tow to tired paddlers before they become completely exhausted may avert the need for a more involved rescue. A tow may be also the only way to transport an injured paddler. Be aware that towlines can become garrotes in the surf zone, where simpler methods should be used.

I prefer a tow system consisting of a quick-release belt on your PFD, a 3' shock-loaded tether and a carabiner, and a separate throw bag with a carabiner. The shock-tether dampens the effects of waves and the throw bag line keep boats from crashing together. A buckle is

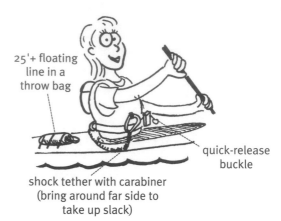

25'+ floating line in a throw bag

quick-release buckle

shock tether with carabiner (bring around far side to take up slack)

only quick-release if you have practiced using it. If you are getting jerked around by the waves, adjust the length of your towline to match the wavelengths so both boats are on the same face of the waves.

The Push-Tow

Use the short tether to retrieve lost boats or to push-tow someone. For a push-tow, face the other person and hold onto each other's bows. Clip your elastic tether to the bow of the other boat and instruct him to push your bow toward his knees, stretching the tether. You can now paddle forward normally because the tether keeps his bow from drifting out and into your way. If the other person should capsize, you are in position to perform an Eskimo Bow Rescue. In an emergency, you can make do without the elastic tether.

The In-Line Tow

Carabiner your elastic tether to the throw bag line, then carabiner this line to the bow of the boat you want to tow. The persons being towed should help paddle if possible. If they feel unsteady they can support themselves with a single paddle float, a paddle float on each side of a fixed paddle, or with another paddler who stabilizes their kayak and is towed alongside them. Clip your towline to the paddler being towed in case you switch assistants. You can also have someone tow the tower.

This is not good.

towing in the surf zone

in-line tow

push-tow

Helping Hands

One of the qualities of being a good leader is keeping track of the big picture and utilizing all your resources during a crisis.

Utilizing Other People

Ideally, the group leader should supervise the scene and not become distracted with the details. A helper can help stabilize the primary rescuer during all these rescues. She should come up on the rescuer's side and face the other rescuer. From this position she can help pull the boat or swimmer up on deck and stabilize the rescuer's kayak. Other paddlers not helping directly can clean up the yard sale of gear washed off or out of a kayak, go to shore and boil some water for hot drinks, or signal for additional help.

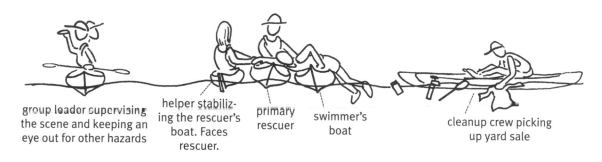

group leader supervising the scene and keeping an eye out for other hazards

helper stabilizing the rescuer's boat. Faces rescuer.

primary rescuer

swimmer's boat

cleanup crew picking up yard sale

Getting Rescued by Others

The first step for getting rescued by others is to leave a float plan with friends. Your float plan should include the following information: name and phone numbers of boaters, number of boats, boat color, route description, itinerary, safety equipment, and the makes, models, and locations of your vehicles.

When you need an extra hand, don't be shy. Get the attention of whomever you can by making yourself bigger, brighter, or different. Tell rescuers where you are, how many are in your group, what your situation is, and how they can help you. Sometimes a boat can help just by shielding you from the wind while you climb back in your boat. Carry all the rescue gizmos you want, but don't rely on them as your sole means to get you out of trouble. Be mindful, creative, and resourceful!

Swims and Rescues — The Race to Get Upright

If you can't get back in your boat, your best option is almost always to stay with your boat because it provides both flotation and visibility. Leaving your boat and swimming for shore is a last option and should be attempted only in the surf or when the shore is extremely close.

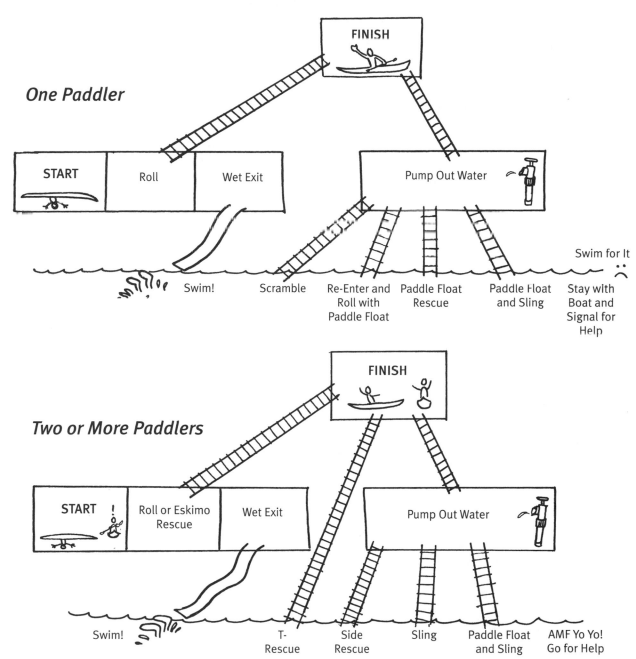

Navigation

"Can't get there from he'ah!"
— BERT AND I

Navigation is physically and mentally connecting the dots from where you are to where you want to go. Paddlers who are a little paranoid about getting lost rarely get lost because they continuously double-check their position. It is usually the paddlers who are overconfident of their position and their navigational ability who lose track of where they are. Know where you are but always maintain a healthy skepticism to keep you on your toes. The classic text on this subject is David Burch's *Fundamentals of Kayak Navigation*.

The Six Mental Stages of Getting Lost

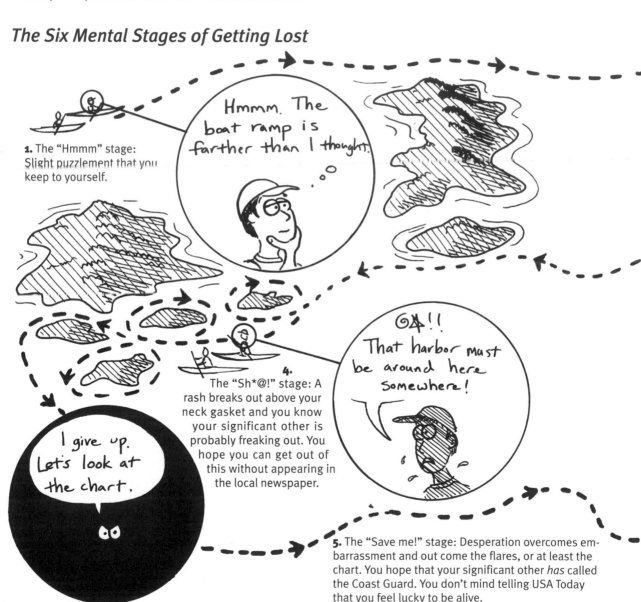

1. The "Hmmm" stage: Slight puzzlement that you keep to yourself.

Hmmm. The boat ramp is farther than I thought.

4. The "Sh*@!" stage: A rash breaks out above your neck gasket and you know your significant other is probably freaking out. You hope you can get out of this without appearing in the local newspaper.

G@!! That harbor must be around here somewhere!

I give up. Let's look at the chart.

5. The "Save me!" stage: Desperation overcomes embarrassment and out come the flares, or at least the chart. You hope that your significant other *has* called the Coast Guard. You don't mind telling *USA Today* that you feel lucky to be alive.

Be Aware Out There

With or without navigational aids, you need to pay attention to your surroundings. Orient yourself at the put-in. Which way is north? Which way is the wind blowing? Where is the sun? Is the current going with you, against you, or across you? Look behind you and make a mental note of the area where you launched. Are there any distinctive trees, houses, rocks, or buoys at the put-in or along the way? Knowing what the skyline looks like can be helpful for late returns.

Check the time you launch so you can estimate your distance the next time you look at your watch. Most folks paddle around 3 miles an hour with no wind or current. If your progress is significantly different than this, figure out why and adjust for the next day's paddle.

Use all your senses along the way. Watch for boat traffic marking shipping lanes and harbor entrances. Sniff for guano from bird colonies and rich ooze from mud flats. Listen for gongs, whistles, horns, and bells from buoys and boats and crashing surf. Feel the wind direction across your face or the cool air of approaching fog.

What to Do When You are Lost

It is better to be standing and lost than swimming and lost. If you are lost and the conditions are deteriorating, go to shore and try to figure out where you are. It may sound obvious, but ask others where you are. Sometimes an exploratory trip around the corner will help pinpoint your position, but avoid a panicked dash that may take you even farther from your float plan (you did remember to leave one, didn't you?).

Ranges ⌁

A range is a staggeringly useful reference line formed when one stationary object is in front of another. You can use a range to monitor your progress in a crossing, locate your position, cordon off a hazardous area, or just stay on course. If the far object moves to the right, you are moving to the right of the line. If the far object moves to the left, you are moving to the left of the line. Practice by putting your nose at the bottom of this page and watch how the mountain peak moves relative to the day marker. By continuously checking ranges you can monitor your progress and tell the moment the tide turns or you've crossed a subtle eddyline. Establish ranges on a chart or map as reference points.

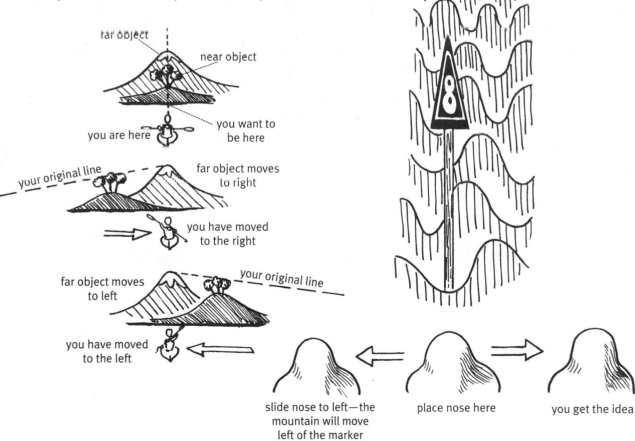

far object

near object

you want to be here

you are here

your original line

far object moves to right

you have moved to the right

far object moves to left

your original line

you have moved to the left

slide nose to left—the mountain will move left of the marker

place nose here

you get the idea

The Range Game

Look at the chart. You are paddling from the bottom of the page toward the top. See if you can identify your position from each view. Answers are on page 125.

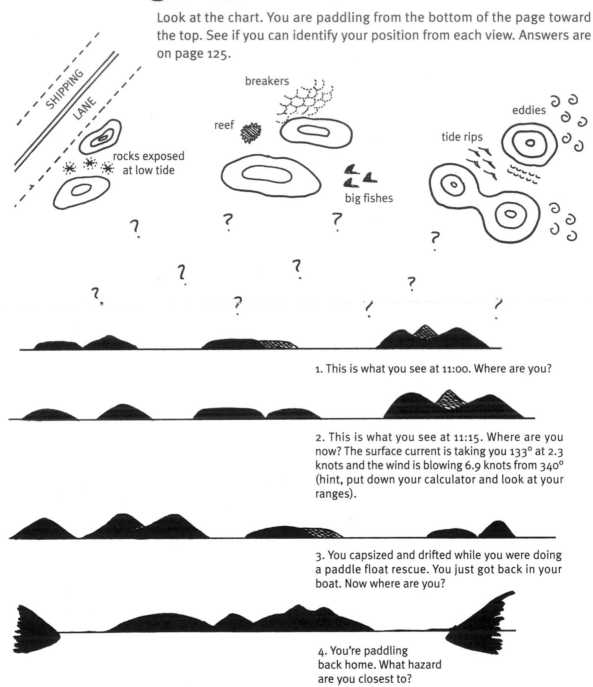

SHIPPING LANE

rocks exposed at low tide

breakers

reef

big fishes

tide rips

eddies

1. This is what you see at 11:00. Where are you?

2. This is what you see at 11:15. Where are you now? The surface current is taking you 133° at 2.3 knots and the wind is blowing 6.9 knots from 340° (hint, put down your calculator and look at your ranges).

3. You capsized and drifted while you were doing a paddle float rescue. You just got back in your boat. Now where are you?

4. You're paddling back home. What hazard are you closest to?

Paddling in a Fog

To paddle in the fog you need a good idea of where you are, where you are going, and when you should be there. In addition to a chart and compass, you should have a sound-producing device that you can blast every two minutes or less to make your presence known to other boaters (listen for the same thing from others!). Hug the shoreline, or, if you're feeling bold, connect the dots between known reference points. Keep away from boat traffic. If you must make a crossing, DON'T aim directly at your destination, but deliberately head to one side so that when you reach the far shore you will know which way to go. When in doubt, trust your compass more than your instinct.

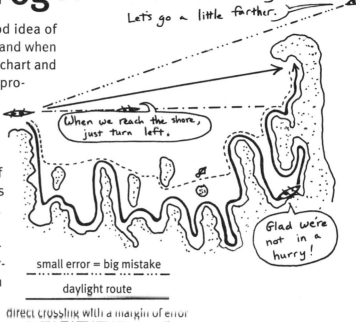

small error = big mistake

daylight route

direct crossing with a margin of error

connecting the dots

conservative shore hugging

Paddling at Night

I recommend paddling someplace extremely familiar for your nocturnal outings. After the sun sets your local lagoon will be transformed into its mysterious and eerie alter ego. If you want to go for a moonlit paddle, schedule your float for a day or two days before the full moon so you will have moonlight as soon as the sun sets. To help navigate at night, use the North Star (Polaris) as a reference in addition to your compass.

You are required to have a bright waterproof white light to alert other boats of your presence. Cyalume lightsticks attached on the back of PFDs or hats will help your group keep track of each other. You will also need a whistle and a visual emergency distress signal such as a strobe, SOS distress light, or three flares.

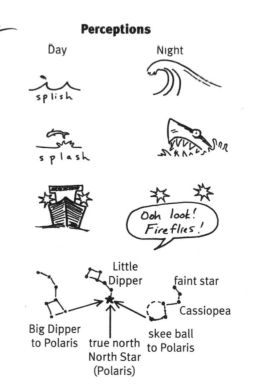

Perceptions

Day — splish

Night

splash

Ooh look! Fireflies!

Little Dipper

faint star

Cassiopea

Big Dipper to Polaris

true north North Star (Polaris)

skee ball to Polaris

Charts and Maps

All these features are helpful only if you know where they are relative to where you want to go. Charts and maps show handy reference points you can follow to your destination. Nautical charts provide more details in and under the water while topographic maps provide more details above the water. Add notes on your chart about good campsites, landmarks, and places to avoid. Your local boating shop will be able to tell you which maps and charts are most helpful for the waters you intend to paddle.

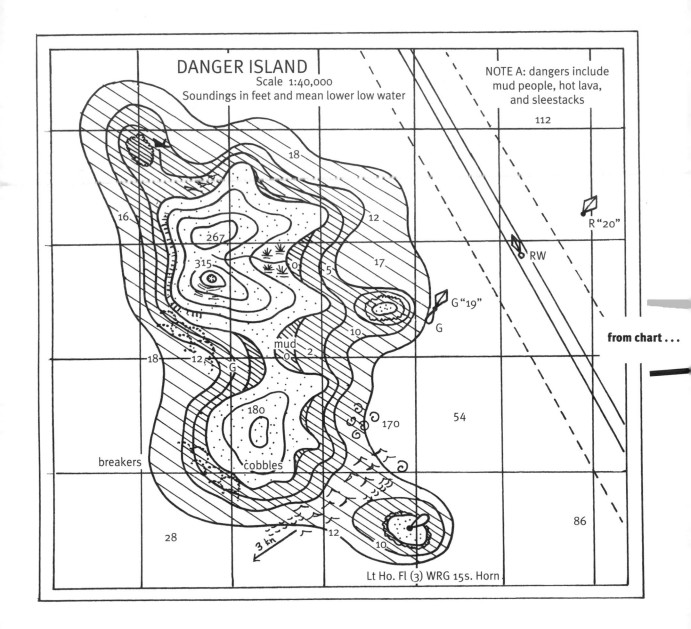

from chart . . .

When to Use Them

Looking at your chart once you are lost is like putting your skirt on once your boat is full of water. If you wait until you really need it, it's too late. Use your chart before your trip to plan camps, find interesting routes, avoid hazards, and identify emergency exits. At the start of the trip identify the key features from shore to accustom yourself to the scale of the chart and check your chart frequently along the way. Whenever you round a bend or enter a harbor, consult the chart and match features you see with symbols on the chart. Fold your charts into a chart case or several zippered plastic bags for use on the water.

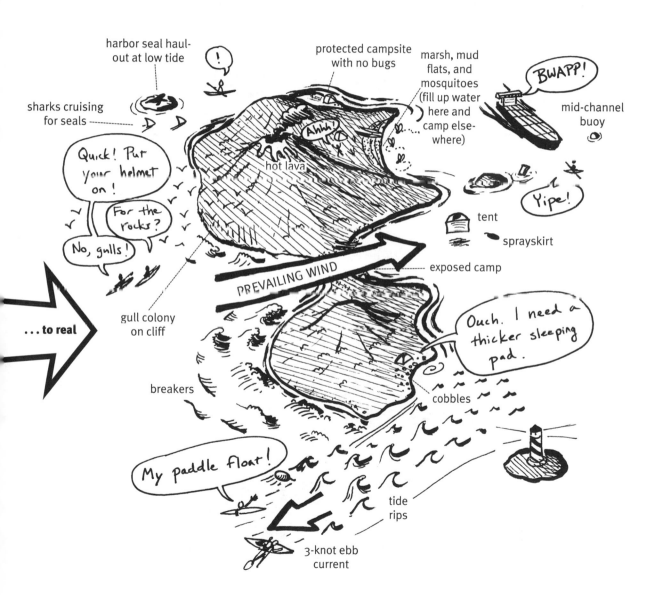

River Maps

When floating a river, you know you are somewhere on a squiggly line, but where? In addition to noticing distinctive features such as bridges, towns, and rapids, keep track of tributaries and bends in the river. In canyon country, inspect the contour lines to see if the wash actually reaches the river level or is a hanging valley far above you. As always, keep track of the time and estimate time traveled downstream (about 3 miles an hour with moderate current). Distinct geologic layers or outcrops described in guidebooks may also pinpoint your position. Use a compass to measure the bearing of a straightaway or the center of a river bend.

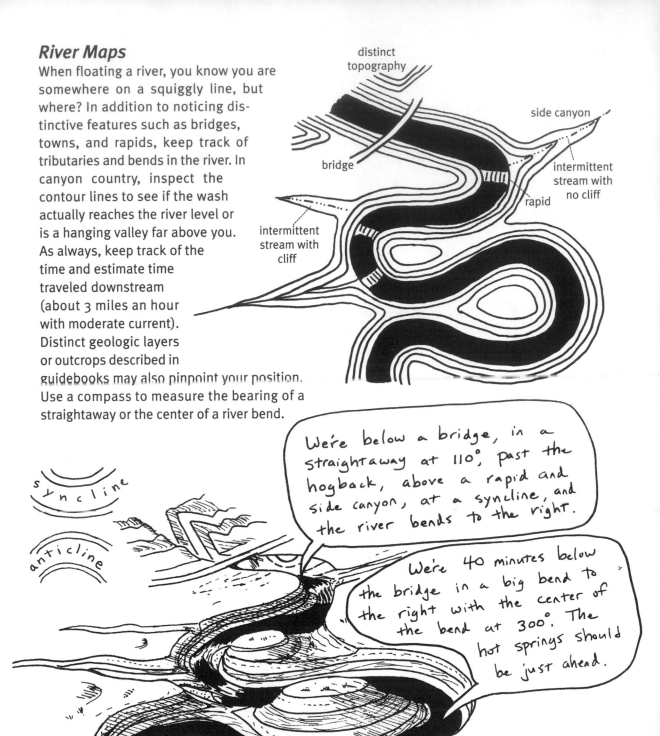

distinct topography

side canyon

bridge

intermittent stream with no cliff

rapid

intermittent stream with cliff

syncline

anticline

We're below a bridge, in a straightaway at 110°, past the hogback, above a rapid and side canyon, at a syncline, and the river bends to the right.

We're 40 minutes below the bridge in a big bend to the right with the center of the bend at 300°. The hot springs should be just ahead.

300°

Scale

A chart with the wrong scale is like a tent with the wrong poles, usable but inconvenient. Distances on topographic maps are shown with a linear scale just like a road map. The scale on charts is built into the vertical border because one minute (1') of latitude equals a nautical mile (6,080 feet).

Scale is also represented as a ratio next to the title, such as 1:40,000. Think of the second number as your elevation above the water. The higher you go the smaller the ground looks and the smaller the scale. A small scale of 1:100,000 gives you an all-commanding view of the coastline but without any useful details. A large scale of 1:1,250 gives you a larger picture of a more limited area. Because kayaks like to dink around a lot and don't cover as many miles as cruise ships, scales of 1:40,000 or larger (more detail) are preferable.

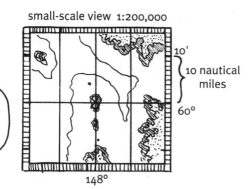

small-scale view 1:200,000

10'
10 nautical miles
60°
148°

When the scale is small you seem quite tall!

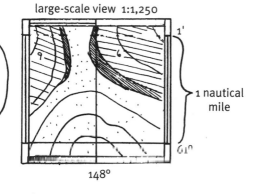

large-scale view 1:1,250

1'
1 nautical mile
61°
148°

When the scale is large you can see the barge!

Symbols

Learn to recognize useful symbols such as buoy types, tide rips, eddies, breakers, mud flats, and rapids. The symbols for US charts are described in Chart No. 1 published by NOAA (National Oceanographic and Atmospheric Administration) and viewable at that website. *Topographic Map Symbols* is a free pamflet published by the US Geological Survey and is also viewable at that website. Details on buoys are given in the *Light List,* published by the US Coast Guard.

Contour lines reflect the topography both above and below the water. Contour lines angle around drainages and ridges in V-shaped curves, with the Vs pointing uphill for drainages and downhill for ridges. Look at special notes on the chart for tips about whether you'll be sleeping on boulders or sand and information about rough water, currents, and traffic.

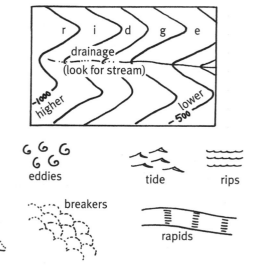

r i d g e
drainage (look for stream)
-1000 higher
lower -500

eddies

tide

rips

breakers

rapids

buoy

cliff

reefs exposed at low tide

mud flats exposed at low tide

Using a Compass

If you see something that appears on the chart and paddle up to it, you know where you are. If that object isn't in your path, you can still find out where you are relative to that object by taking a bearing with a compass. A bearing is simply a line from that object back to you, measured in degrees from true or magnetic north. The difference between true north and magnetic north varies regionally and is called the declination on topo maps and variation on charts.

Charts show true north and magnetic north on the outer and inner rings of the compass rose, respectively, and depict true north in lines of longitude across the chart. Topographic maps show true north and magnetic north with a declination diagram in the map margin and true north with lines of longitude (also known as meridians).

true ★ north

compass rose (chart)

TN ★   MN

20°

declination diagram (topo map)

Deck compass: point your bow to what you want to measure

read labels from lubber line (usually on near side)

Hand compass: point the compass at what you want to measure

first turn housing until arrow matches needle, then read numbers from index line on far side

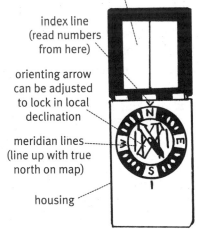

Hand compass with declination adjustment: optional mirror to see if arrow is underneath needle

index line (read numbers from here)

orienting arrow can be adjusted to lock in local declination

meridian lines (line up with true north on map)

housing

The type of compass you have will determine if you should measure a bearing from magnetic north or true north. If you have a marine compass or a basic backpacking compass, measure everything from magnetic north (the inner compass rose or declination arrow). If you have a fancy hiking compass set for the declination (see the directions), measure everything from true north (outer compass rose or longitude).

If you have a deck-mounted compass, point your boat at the object. If you have a handheld compass, point your compass at the object and rotate the housing until the orienting arrow lies directly beneath the needle. Read the bearing between you and the object marked by the index line.

Using Magnetic North

Hikers waste whole days trying to convert between magnetic north and true north, so skip that step and measure everything in magnetic north.

1. Look for a distinctive object, identify it on the chart, and take a bearing to it.

2. Lay a straightedge on the chart's compass rose at that same angle on the magnetic north ring.

3. Without losing that angle, shift your straightedge so it lines up with the object on the chart. (A plotter, a clear plastic sheet with parallel lines is helpful for this part.) You now know you are somewhere on that line.

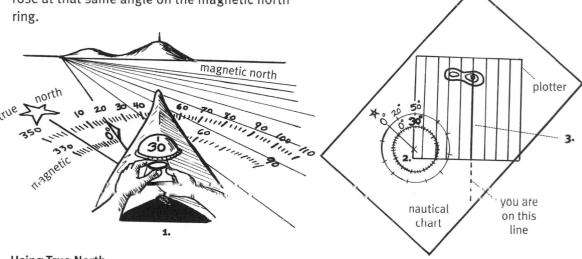

Using True North

If you have an expensive compass that adjusts for the declination, skip the parallel ruler–compass rose funny business and base all your measurements from true north (a line of longitude). Once you have your bearing (1), forget about the needle and use your compass as a protractor to measure the angle you just recorded. Lay the compass near your object with the meridian lines (the parallel black lines inside the housing) lined up with a longitude line on the map or chart (2). Slide the compass up or down this line until the edge of the compass rests against your object (3). Know you are somewhere on that line.

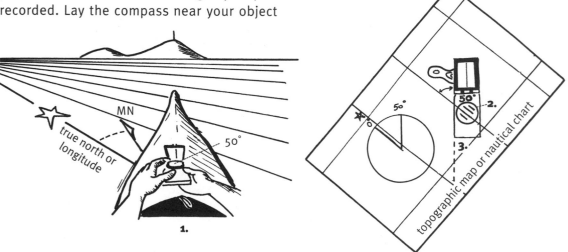

Find a Fix to Prevent Getting in a Fix

To find out where you are on that line, take additional bearings. A fix is the intersection of two or more lines indicating your probable position. A third bearing will form a "cocked hat" or triangle. While you can be anywhere in that triangle, imagine yourself in the corner closest to danger so you will err on the side of safety. Since a river is also a line on a map, you only need one other bearing to fix your position.

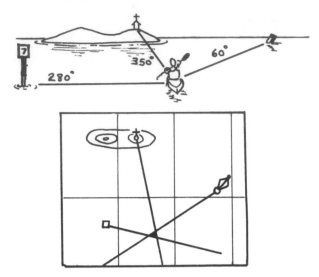

Plotting a Course

To find your way through island mazes, deceptive points, and swirls of fog, first plot a course on your map and then follow it with your compass. 1. Place your compass or plotter from where you are to where you want to go. 2. If you are using true north, turn the compass housing so the meridian lines are lined up with true north (longitude) and read the angle. If you are using magnetic north, use a plotter to read the angle on the inner ring of the compass rose. 3. Turn your boat so the red orienting arrow stays beneath the needle or the lubber line stays on your course and follow that bearing toward your destination. Establish a front range to stay on course and a side range to monitor your progress. Compensate for winds and currents as needed. The night before a predawn crossing, set your compass or make a note of your intended course while you can still see.

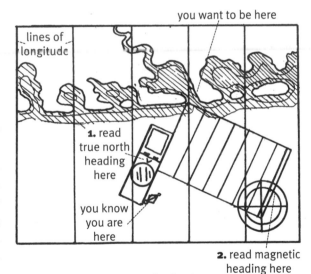

GPS Units and Other Gadgetry

Gearheads will be thrilled with fancy GPS units that can display your position relative to specific buoys and the coastline. Electronic navigation systems make a wonderful complement to a chart and compass, but don't rely on them exclusively.

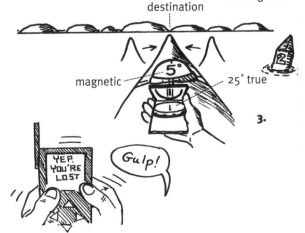

Traffic

Rules of the Road

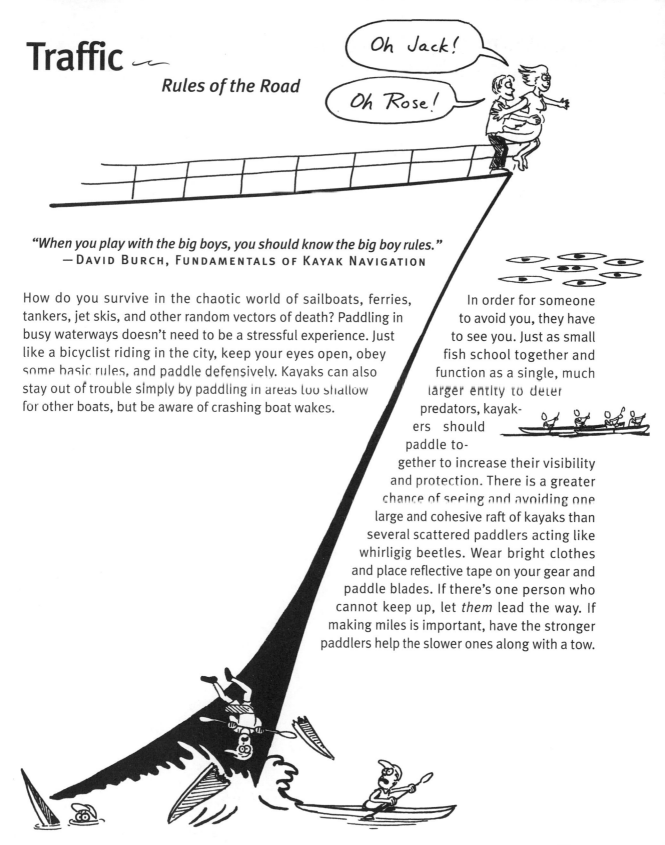

"When you play with the big boys, you should know the big boy rules."
— DAVID BURCH, FUNDAMENTALS OF KAYAK NAVIGATION

How do you survive in the chaotic world of sailboats, ferries, tankers, jet skis, and other random vectors of death? Paddling in busy waterways doesn't need to be a stressful experience. Just like a bicyclist riding in the city, keep your eyes open, obey some basic rules, and paddle defensively. Kayaks can also stay out of trouble simply by paddling in areas too shallow for other boats, but be aware of crashing boat wakes.

In order for someone to avoid you, they have to see you. Just as small fish school together and function as a single, much larger entity to deter predators, kayakers should paddle together to increase their visibility and protection. There is a greater chance of seeing and avoiding one large and cohesive raft of kayaks than several scattered paddlers acting like whirligig beetles. Wear bright clothes and place reflective tape on your gear and paddle blades. If there's one person who cannot keep up, let *them* lead the way. If making miles is important, have the stronger paddlers help the slower ones along with a tow.

Hit or Miss? The Bow Angle Method

The bow angle method tells you if another boat is going to pass in front of you, behind you, or right over you. Let's say you're going for a nice paddle in Loch Ness. Note the beastie's position relative to your bow, with your bow being 12:00. Watch how its position changes over a few seconds while you both maintain your course and speed. If it moves closer to your bow it will pass in front of you. If it moves closer to your stern, it will pass behind. If the angle to the vessel doesn't change you are on a colli-

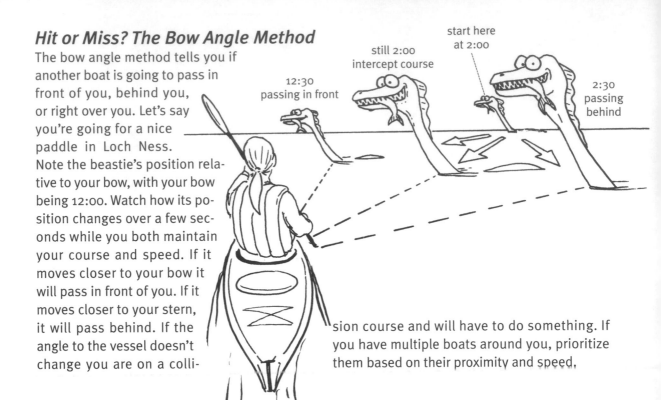

12:30 passing in front

still 2:00 intercept course

start here at 2:00

2:30 passing behind

sion course and will have to do something. If you have multiple boats around you, prioritize them based on their proximity and speed,

Shipping Lanes

If shipping lanes are the aquatic equivalent of the Autobahn, kayaks rank somewhere between squirrels and opossums. Ships with deep drafts have to stay within these deep channels, so they have the right of way over everything else. Know where shipping lanes are, recognize buoys, and be aware of turns and intersections in these lanes. Remember that boats heading back to port keep red buoys on their right side, thus the mnemonic "red, right, returning." Minimize your time in shipping lanes by crossing them at right angles when there is a break in the traffic.

Playing Chicken

If you are not in a shipping lane and the other vessel is coming straight toward you, both you and the oncoming vessel should veer to the right.

Passing from Behind

If another vessel is coming up directly behind you, it's just like when a faster skier passes you on a cat track. Hold your course and speed so the other boat can steer around you without worrying about any sudden moves you might make. If you try to dodge them at the last minute, you might fling yourself in their path. If you think they might not see you, take evasive maneuvers.

passing vessel must maneuver around

burdened vessel maintaining course

There's a boat behind us! Which way should we move?

Stay on target... Stay on target!

Evasive Maneuvers

Being on a collision course with a boat coming from any other angle than directly in front or behind is just like two cars coming to a four-way stop at the same time. Ideally, the person on the right has the right of way and the other person should alter course to pass behind. In reality, the more maneuverable and more squishable vessel (usually the kayak) should yield to the less maneuverable and heavier vessel (everything else). Make eye contact with the captain (not just the passengers) and make obvious adjustments in your course and speed so the crew on the other vessel sees that you have seen them. Don't play squirrel and make them guess where you're going. Avoid incremental adjustments in your steering or speed that might be clear to you but not to them.

BEEP! BEEP!

I've got to fake this thing out!

Left, no, right! The current's going left but the wind going right...

BWAP! BWAP! BWAP! BWAP! BWAP!

When a Collision Seems Imminent

You may be in the middle of a rescue, towing another kayak, or in need of rescuing yourself when you look up to see a boat bearing down on you. One long horn blast from an approaching vessel means that you are in the way. Five short blasts mean that you are on the way to becoming a speed bump. No blasts mean they probably haven't seen you. Let them know you are there by waving your paddle vigorously, blowing your whistle, or even firing a flare. Hopefully the person on watch will look down and be able to make a last-minute change in course.

If a collision seems imminent, keep sprinting in the safest direction. If you get hit by the other boat, use your kayak as some sort of protection, and tuck to protect your head. If you are out of your boat, swim away as fast as possible. Once you reach the surface, look for others in your group and flag down help. Screaming is perfectly appropriate at this time.

Personal Watercraft

On a serious note about sharing waterways, be respectful of everyone out there, even jet skis. Smile, wave, and be a good ambassador for the sport of kayaking. Personal watercraft can make excellent rescue vehicles as long as you didn't flip them off earlier. If you see reckless behavior, report it to the proper authorities. The Bluewater network (www.bluewaternetwork.org) is an organization that works to restrict improper personal watercraft use from sensitive waters.

Range Game Answer Key

Hold this page upside down and in front of a mirror for the answers.
See page 112.

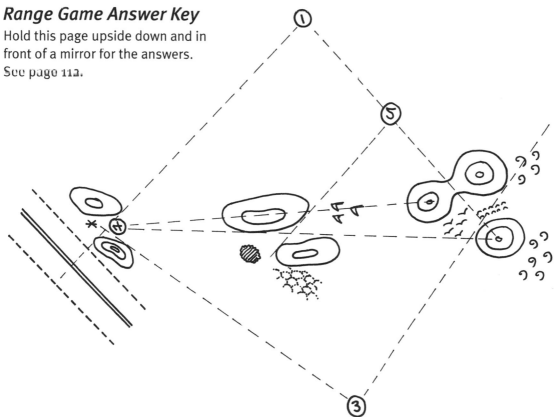

Wind and Waves

ENERGY

weathercocking (turning upwind)

3 2 1

cat's paws

chop

white caps

While sunshine and temperature have tremendous psychological effects on kayakers, wind has the most direct physical effect. Wind is the roundabout transfer of sunlight energy from hot places to cold places. Although air is less dense than water, most of your kayak and body is in the air (you hope). The wind can have an over-riding effect and can effectively convert your kayak into a kite.

In addition to blowing kayaks around, the wind also sweeps up water molecules into cat's paws or ripples, which meld together to form sets of waves. Waves absorb the wind energy of huge storms spanning hundreds of miles, and over time sort themselves by wavelength into silent swells. These swells release a concentrated version of the storm in the surf zone. The size of waves is determined by the strength of the wind, the length of time it blows, and

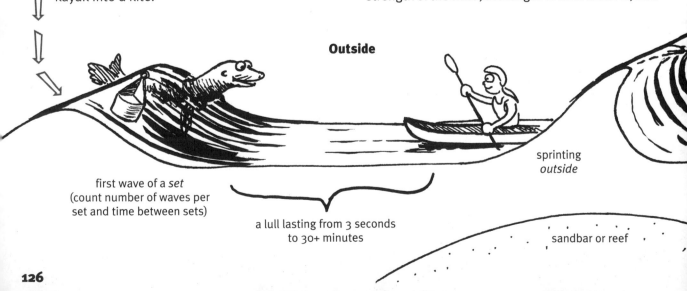

Outside

first wave of a *set*
(count number of waves per
set and time between sets)

a lull lasting from 3 seconds
to 30+ minutes

sprinting
outside

sandbar or reef

the fetch or distance the wind travels over water. Waves may be generated by localized squalls (wind waves) or by storms thousands of miles away (swells). Interacting with waves is one of the best reasons to kayak, as you shall see.

127

Wind

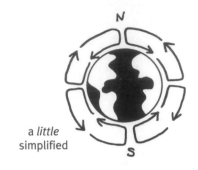

a *little* simplified

Where the Wind Comes From

Where sunlight hits the Earth's surface, the air expands and rises, creating an area of low pressure. The atmosphere re-radiates the heat back to outer space, air shrinks and falls back down in a different place, forming an area of high pressure. As these air masses move up and down they suck nearby air inward and concentrate energy (low pressure) or blow air outward, dispersing this energy (high pressure).

Forecasting

Despite weather being one of the most unpredictable systems on earth, you can make some generalizations based on the barometric pressure, temperature, wind speed, wind direction, and cloud composition. Learn the local weather patterns by listening to the marine forecast on the weather radio and hanging with locals in the bars. Be sure to listen to the forecast over the next 12, 24, and 48 hours, as systems may move in suddenly.

Land and Sea Breezes

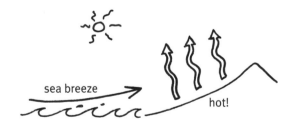

Because it takes more energy to heat water than rocks, the air above the land heats up more quickly than the air above the sea. The rising air above the land creates a region of low pressure, and the air over the ocean moves inland to replace it. This is why onshore breezes and upriver winds are common during the day. At night the situation is reversed because the land cools more quickly than the water. The air over the land sinks and drains back toward the ocean, forming an offshore or downriver wind in the evening.

Paddling in the Wind

Paddling into headwinds is like driving a car on a washboard road, because it slows you down and tires you out. Tail winds can provide a nice push and can stir up some waves to surf you on your way. There are many excellent saling rigs for kayaks, or you can make use of a tarp or umbrella. Crosswinds push you to the side and tend to turn your kayak upwind if you are paddling forward, an annoying habit known as weathercocking. Adjust your paddling plan and exit points carefully anytime the wind gusts over 15 mph or blows against strong currents. Empty kayaks are tossed around more than loaded kayaks, so consider securing some ballast in your boat for less skittering.

Weathercocking

bow wedged by bow wake, kayak turns upwind

upwind sweep (horizontal sweep); upwind lean

vertical stroke on downwind side; no lean

As you paddle forward your bow is pinned in place by your bow wave while your stern is free to waggle. A gust from the side slides your stern downwind faster than your bow, making your kayak turn upwind. Slow your stern's sideways drift by placing more of it underwater. Deploy a skeg or rudder or sink it more than the bow with lots of gear in that end. You can also use a wider stroke on the upwind side and a vertical stroke on the downwind side. The coolest way to stay on track is to time your strokes so that on every windward stroke you also tilt your boat to windward. An upwind boat lean and forward sweep will turn your boat downwind.

If you are stuck sideways in the wind and cannot turn, let the wind weathercock your boat in the direction you want to go. Paddle forward to turn upwind and backward to turn downwind.

To prevent a gust of wind from snatching your paddle away, keep your paddle blade low in strong winds. If the wind does catch the underside of your blade and is about to toss you over, let go with your windward hand and reposition your paddle.

Waves ~

Avoiding waves in a capable sea kayak is like not driving your Extrema SUV on a dirt road. Sea kayaks may be safe on car tops and in harbors, but that's not what sea kayaks are for. Being comfortable paddling in moderate waves lets you have tremendous fun, extends your paddling possibilities tremendously, and is excellent practice for coping with adverse conditions.

fun meter

no harbor needed

no worries mate

How Waves Move

As the deep roots of waves start dragging in shallow water, the waves slow down. If the bottom is uneven or the wave approaches at an angle, the section of the wave still in deep water will keep speeding ahead and make the wavefronts bend or refract around the shoreline. When waves pass around an island, they wrap around the island until they meet on the other side and pass through each other. Wave refraction is especially apparent at headlands and bays. Like sunlight through a magnifying glass, wave energy is focused and concentrated at headlands and dispersed when entering bays.

Even with wave refraction, the initial angle of a swell has a tremendous effect on how they reach the beach. A beach directly facing the incoming swell may have huge surf, while a neighboring beach facing a different angle or protected by a headland may have much smaller waves. Offshore kelp beds can help reduce the wind chop in incoming waves.

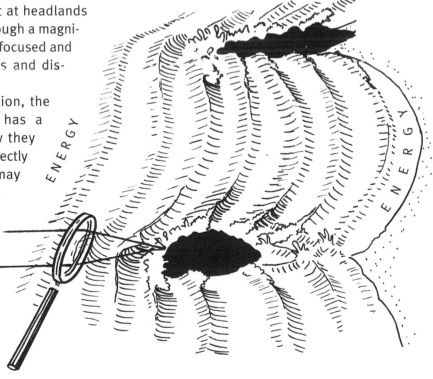

ENERGY

ENERGY

ENERGY

How Waves Are Measured

It is ALWAYS bigger when you get out there. Use extra caution when checking out the surf from parking lots perched high above the surf. Use binoculars and look for objects to use for scale. Think twice about paddling where the waves are described as heavy, thick, sick, gnarly, pitching, pumping, going off, or sucking dry. Mushy, crumbling, and mellow describe milder conditions. It's better to go out when it's too small than too big.

Parking Lot Perspective	Reality Check
Wow! It's huge!	You won't even make it outside, and if you do, you won't want to be there.
Looks fun!	An epic day. Be sure you write your phone number on your boat and paddle.
Huh. Well, it's better than nothing.	Perfect conditions. You'll want your photo in Patagonia.
It's sooooo flat!	Excellent for taking your friends out for their first surf session.

How Waves Break

deep open water   wave   bottom shape   shore

It is extremely important to pay attention to how waves break around you because that determines what options you have for landing, launching, surfing, or touring. Just like a mountain biker hitting a rock and crashing, waves cruise blissfully through the ocean until they hit shallow water, wipe out, and break. The shape of the bottom determines the way a wave wipes out. When you paddle in the surf, you are entering that wipe-out zone. Waves may change from one type to another as they reform and reshape in the surf zone or as the tide changes the profile of the bottom. Subtle changes in the slope of a beach can make waves spill in one place and surge a few yards away.

Plunging (Hawaii 5-O) Waves

Plunging waves abruptly hit a steep, shallow reef or beach and do the classic end-over-end wipeout. As their crest pitches out over the rest of the wave, they temporarily form a barrel, also known as a tube or "the green room." These waves are incredibly violent and powerful and only experienced kayakers should attempt surfing them. Beware getting sucked back "over the falls" when paddling out through these waves. These waves are much more dangerous than surging waves when they break directly on rocks or a beach.

steep rise = plunging wave

Spilling Waves

Like a mountain biker dabbing left, then right, and losing a water bottle before finally sliding out, spilling waves lose their energy gradually. The wave crest crumbles into foam without forming a tube. This is the best type of wave for sea kayak surfing (see next chapter). Because of the shallow beach profile needed to form these waves, the surf zone often extends far offshore and it may be a long paddle outside. These waves often re-form inside, sometimes as plunging or surging waves.

gently sloping bottom = spilling wave

Surging Waves

To simulate a surging wave, ride a mountain bike straight up a steep hill or skateboard ramp, stall out, and slide back down without toppling over. The advantage of these waves is that if the shoreline is steep enough, you can paddle right next to rocks or cliffs without having any whitewater wash you against them. The disadvantage is that because no energy has been dissipated before the wave hits the shore, surging waves wash up with unexpected force and distance. Surging waves are notoriously difficult to land in because you tend to slide back down the steep beach into the maw of the next wave. Let your friends land first so they can hold your boat for you. Beware that bigger waves or a sloping bottom will cause waves to break instead of surge!

very steep beaches, rocks, and bridge pilings = surging waves

Surf Zone Currents

The surf zone is one of the most dynamic environments on the planet. In addition to the aforementioned wave types, there are several other features that kayakers need to be aware of.

Littoral Currents

Littoral currents are created when waves wash up and down a beach diagonally and move water parallel with the beach. When you are in your kayak you may feel that you are in the same place, but a quick look behind you will show that you are drifting. This current may not be as strong outside the surf zone.

Rip Currents

Rip currents (inappropriately called rip tides) are currents that head straight out to sea from the beach. They form when water piled up from waves becomes dammed up behind a sandbar. Where there is a low spot in the sandbar, the excess water pours back out to sea and further erodes this channel. This current then dissipates beyond the surf zone. Rip tides may create a distinct surface texture in the surf zone because wind and waves have a different effect on the outgoing water. Smaller waves may not break in the channel, and there may be a visible cloud of suspended sediment in the outgoing flow. Rip tides are hazardous for swimmers but helpful for kayaks, because they can serve as a convenient conveyer belt back outside. If you find yourself swimming in a rip current, swim across the channel to the sandbar from where you can swim back to shore, but be careful of littoral currents that may sweep you back into the rip. Another option is to float out with the rip current until it dissipates, then swim parallel to shore and come in across the sandbar where the waves are breaking. Rip currents often form along headlands, breakwaters, jetties, and piers.

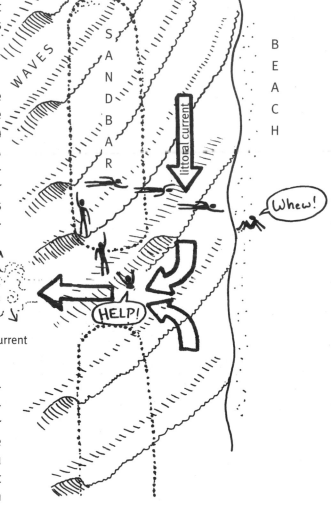

rip current

Launching in Waves
Site Selection

Choosing an appropriate launching site is a crit-ical skill. A safe, low-energy site will usually have a gently sloping beach, fine sand, small spilling waves, few people, and no obvious ob-structions or hazards. Looking at the size of the sand at the water's edge can give you an idea of the wave history of the beach: the larger the sediment, the stronger the energy. Before you launch, be sure to secure your rudder and any items you don't want to donate to the deep.

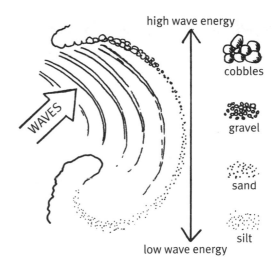

Getting to the Water

The easiest way to launch is to have someone drag you out until you can float. To avoid getting left high and dry or swamped, watch several waves and see how high an average wave washes up the beach. When you see another set of average-sized waves coming (no lulls or big sets) drag your boat down to the same height and sit on the back of your cockpit. The next wave should reach your feet without float-ing your kayak. Keep your feet out to keep you from washing out to sea prematurely. Wash the sand off your booties in the backwash and then climb in and secure your sprayskirt before the next wave comes. If you are lucky, the next wave should float you enough so you can reach deep water with some gorilla scoots.

gorilla scoot

Punching Out Through Waves

Timing is the next critical step for successful launching. Wait in the soup zone for a lull to sprint out between sets of waves. Adjust your position between the impact zone and beach break by paddling forward and backward as needed. Never paddle out directly behind another boat.

Momentum is the key for getting outside, so paddle hard. For waves that are chest high or smaller, reach over the back of the wave and pull your kayak through. For larger waves, try to meet the wave either before or after it breaks. Build up as much speed as you can and then tuck forward and spear it with your paddle off to the side. As you pass through the wave, paddle forward to keep your momentum going. Waves can take longer to break than you think, so it may be better to go for it than hesitate and

have it break on your head. When in doubt, stroke it out.

For giant waves that jack up when you've almost made it outside, choose between a fight or flight response. To fight your way outside, take several strong strokes for momentum, tuck forward and flip over so the crest lands on your hull instead of your head, then roll back up in the soup once the wave has passed you. Even if you don't have a roll, at least you will go out on your own terms. To flee, turn around or backpaddle to shore. The broken wave will catch up with you and surf you back to the beach, but at least you might still be in your boat.

If you flip over sideways in the surf, the waves will almost right your kayak in a maneuver called a barrel roll. All you need to do is be

set up for a roll on the correct side. This is where knowing how to roll on both sides comes in handy. If you are disoriented, stay tucked and feel which way the water drags your body and set your paddle up on that side. If you can only roll on one side and it's not with the wave, stay tucked until the wave washes over you.

Once you've made it outside, make sure you really *are* outside by paddling another fifty yards or so before you catch your breath. Set up several ranges to pinpoint your position both up the beach and off the shore. Now you can surf, fish, go for a pleasant paddle, or just enjoy the swells.

setting up ranges

Paddling in Waves

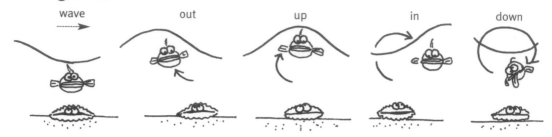

wave   out   up   in   down

Paddling in waves is different from paddling in wind because the surface of the water moves in several directions, not just one. As a wave passes under your kayak, your boat is dragged out, up, in, and down to where you started. When multiple waves from multiple sources collide they create confused and chaotic seas for kayakers. If you need to change directions and the wind isn't too strong, turn on top of a wave crest when both ends of your kayak are out of the water (1).

2. If you paddle directly against waves, your kayak will accelerate as you go down into the trough and slow down at the crest. If waves keep landing on your lap, punch through the waves at an angle or slow down a bit.

3. If you paddle at an angle to the waves, oncoming crests nudge your kayak sideways while troughs stretch your kayak out between waves. Your bow will waggle back and forth but your course should even out.

4. If you paddle directly across waves, keep your hips loose and be ready to tilt your boat into a broken wave face.

5. If you paddle with the waves, the forward motion of the wave crests will help push you along but the backward motion of the trough will slow you down. If you can paddle fast enough to stay on the face of the wave, gravity will slide you down the wave (dude!). Be aware that waves can push your stern faster than your bow, in which case your stern will catch up with your bow and turn your kayak sideways into a broach (6) or potentially end over end. To avoid going vertical with an ender, steer to the side to keep your bow from submerging (pearling) and lean back. These events can be casual or catastrophic, depending on whether you have read the next section or not.

swell #1   swell #2

wind chop

Landing in the Surf Zone

Landing gracefully in the surf is like snowboarding down the ski hill, down a set of stairs, and across the parking lot to your car. A lot can happen along the way. Choose your landing site carefully. Steer clear of surfers, swimmers, and waders. Because conditions change constantly, the site you launched from may no longer be an option, so have a backup plan in mind. Send a guinea pig in ahead to find a good spot to land and warn any swimmers of the approaching chaos (see paddle signals on page 60).

Option #1. Wait for a Lull Between the Sets and Sprint for Shore.

Advantages: No messing about with bracing in the whitewater. You can paddle straight up the beach if your timing is right.

Disadvantages: The timing is never right. Waves travel much faster than your kayak and you will need to deal with the whitewater.

Option #2. Catch a Wave, Wait for It to Break, and Side-Surf It In.

Advantages: This is a free ride in because the wave does most of the work. Also, this is what usually happens anyway. Just as a shopping cart inevitably veers into your car door, your kayak will turn sideways on a broken wave. You can use a stern pry when you first catch a wave to turn yourself toward one side or another, but the wave makes the final call. As soon as you know which direction you are turning, tilt your

boat into the wave, keep your head centered over the boat, stabilize yourself with a brace, and enjoy the ride.

Disadvantages: Beginning paddlers often try to steer when they are already sidesurfing, which is one of the most dynamic ways to flip over. Leaning away from the wave or not leaning at all is akin to catching your downhill edge when skiing or snowboarding. But don't lean your head and body into the wave either. Too much weight on your brace will cause you to fall into the wave as the foam pile subsides. The answer is to use a J-lean (p. 56) to keep your edge up and your boat balanced.

Must... try... to... turn... AHHH!

WHAM!

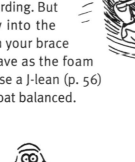

no weight on paddle

edge up

head not over boat

too much weight

lean into wave early

head balanced over butt

Option #3. Catch a Wave and Ride in on Top of the Foam Pile.

Advantages: By paddling forward and backward as needed, you can stay balanced on the forward edge of the top of the foam pile, paddle straight up on the beach with the surge, and hop out of the boat.

Disadvantages: If your timing is off, you will slide ahead or behind the wave, resulting in options #1, #2, or #4.

Option #4. Flip Spectacularly and Swim In.

Advantages: This is a good backup plan if all the other options fail.

Disadvantages: This landing increases the chances for gear and bodily damage, particularly if you get between your boat and the shore. Duck under your boat or quickly move to the side before a breaker hits it. Holding onto your boat in the surf zone is usually not as crucial as in open water and can be downright dangerous in bigger breakers. Push your boat in front of you instead of pulling it in behind you. Don't wrap your hands or fingers around grab loops or deck lines. If you become separated from your boat, it will usually find its way to shore before you do. To hitch a ride on your boat or another boat as it side-surfs in, hold onto the cockpit or hull and ride it like a boogie board. Empty the water

by rolling your boat upside down or using the Flip and Drip method (see Rescues, p. 80) before you try to drag it up the beach.

What to Do When You Reach the Shore

Any surf landing you can walk away from is a good one. The hardest part is often exiting your boat before the next wave comes. Think of it like clipping your biking shoes free from your pedals when you stop before you fall over.

Clear the Runway

If you can't find an area clear of people, one paddler should land carefully and politely ask folks to move to the side for the time being. The person can then direct other boats in one at a time (see Paddle Signals, pp. 60–61). The surf craft controller can also hold boats when they land to keep them from sliding back out to sea. Be aware that a kayak washing up and down the beach acts just like a 17' wide bowling ball and helpers may need fancy footwork.

Straight Landings

Paddle up the beach as far as you can. If you think you can get out before the next wave comes, you can even pop your skirt just before you stop. As soon as your boat stops, hold your paddle to the side or toss it up the beach and hop out. If you start slipping backward, use both your paddle and hand to hold your position until the wave recedes and your boat stops moving. Grab your boat and run up the beach!

Sideways Landings

If you are washing in sideways, you can try to straighten your boat with a forward sweep as the wave settles down. If the bottom of your boat starts catching the sand, use a low brace against the sand to keep yourself upright. If your kayak is beached sideways when the wave recedes, hop out and quickly carry your boat up. Before you slide back down, use your paddle to sweep yourself straight and hold your position with your paddle and hand.

Touch-and-Go Landings

Touch-and-go landings happen when you slide back out into the soup. You may want to paddle clear of the shore break and try to come straight in or wait until a larger wave beaches you.

Turning Around and Doing It Again

To turn back around once you've beached yourself, take a tip from killer whales that surf a wave up a beach, snatch a snoozing sea lion, and turn back around again by arching their back. Simulate this by leaning your boat way over on its side to increase your rocker, then use your hand and paddle to pivot around.

Wake Up!

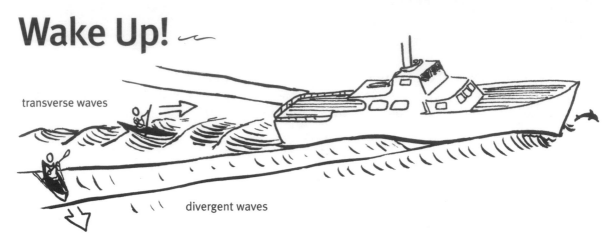

transverse waves

divergent waves

As kayakers living away from open coasts know, you can take advantage of the waves produced by boats, including your own. Stay well out of the way of the wake-producing vessel, and make sure you do not present a hazard to navigation. Be forewarned that the Coast Guard and local police frown on this activity, and with good reason.

Surfing Wakes

As a vessel travels through the water it displaces water in two types of waves. Stern, or transverse, waves pop up immediately behind the vessel and move in its direction, matching its speed. Displacement, or divergent, waves start at the bow, where they are surfed by dolphins. These waves travel outward at a 160° angle and can be surfed by kayaks at a respectful distance. Many ship wakes are not steep enough to catch, but sailboats and powerboats with displacement hulls (and even kayaks) can produce ridable wakes. The steepest waves are found where divergent bow waves intersect transverse waves.

Surfing a stern wave is also known as drafting, because the waves move with the same speed and direction as the boat, propelling you along behind it. To surf a stern wave, ferry out behind the vessel and aim for a wave with a shape that fits your hull. Keep an eye out for boat traffic, and do not try to surf behind military vessels.

Drafting behind a fast-moving kayak is a great way to save energy in races and on long-distance trips. Place your bow directly behind the stern of the lead kayak (the shorter the boat, the closer the distance), and keep it there by paddling on the left when the draftee paddles on the right, and so on. You won't be able to stop paddling completely, but you will save some energy.

Divergent bow waves move away from the source instead of along with it, meaning there's less worry about getting too close or inhaling boat exhaust. To catch a divergent bow wake, position yourself out of the way of boat traffic and perpendicular to the wave (at about 2:00 relative to the boat). As with ocean swells, individual waves move faster than the wave train. To compensate for this, wait for the first five or six waves to pass you and accelerate when your bow drops down into the back of a wave ahead of you. Eventually you will find yourself surfing into the calm water in front of the wave train and will have to wait for the waves to catch up with you again.

To minimize the effect of a wake, turn your kayak head-on and paddle through the series of waves. Beware of waves reflecting from a shore.

drafting

Rock the Boat, Baby: Using Waves of Your Own Making

To find a channel in extremely shallow water, wiggle your hips to send out waves, which will slow down and steepen in the shallowest water but not in the deeper channels.

deeper

shallower

You can gain a few centimeters of clearance in super-shallow water by slowing down so your bow wave passes you, then paddling in on top of it.

Slow down... now speed up

Kayak Surfing

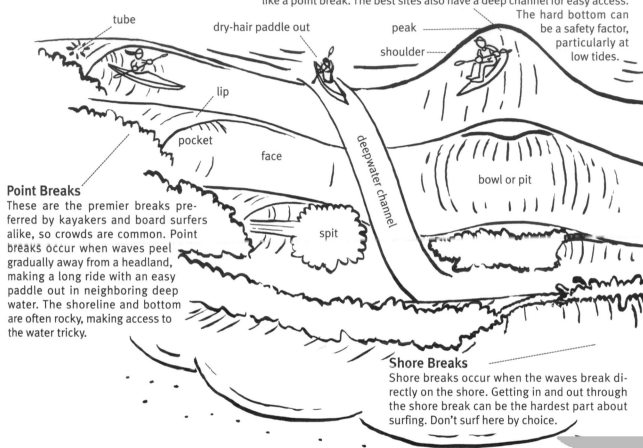

Reef Breaks
Reef breaks occur when waves break on a solid bottom such as a coral reef or rock outcrop. Variations in the bottom may shape a wave so it breaks like a point break. The best sites also have a deep channel for easy access. The hard bottom can be a safety factor, particularly at low tides.

tube

dry-hair paddle out

peak

shoulder

lip

pocket

face

deepwater channel

bowl or pit

Point Breaks
These are the premier breaks preferred by kayakers and board surfers alike, so crowds are common. Point breaks occur when waves peel gradually away from a headland, making a long ride with an easy paddle out in neighboring deep water. The shoreline and bottom are often rocky, making access to the water tricky.

spit

Shore Breaks
Shore breaks occur when the waves break directly on the shore. Getting in and out through the shore break can be the hardest part about surfing. Don't surf here by choice.

Surfing is quite simply the most fun you can have in a kayak. Surfing also improves your paddling skills and self-confidence tremendously. While you can get a push from the forward motion of any wave crest, the real fun starts when the wave is steep enough so your kayak slides downhill on the moving wave face. If you angle your kayak across the wave, you can move much faster than the actual wave front. The surfing tips in this chapter form the building blocks for more advanced surfing maneuvers. The best surfing breaks have waves that peel steadily and predictably from one end of the wave front to the other. The dominant direction that a wave breaks (right or left) is described from the perspective of a person surfing the waves, similar to skier's left or river right. Going left on a wave looks like you are going right from the shore.

Ideally the waves break some distance from shore—so you have some time to enjoy the ride—

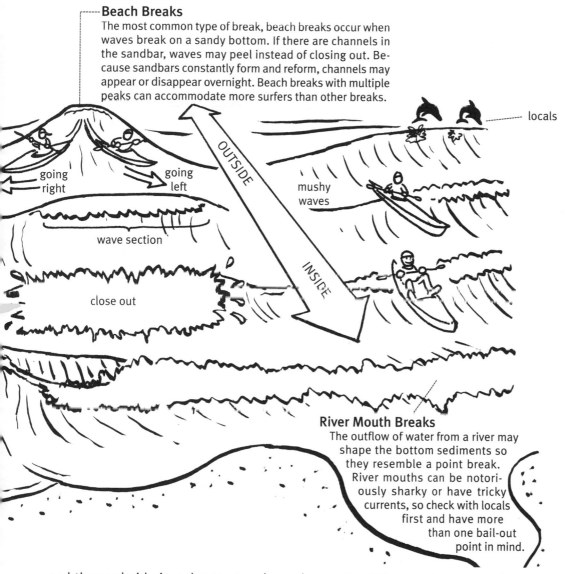

Beach Breaks
The most common type of break, beach breaks occur when waves break on a sandy bottom. If there are channels in the sandbar, waves may peel instead of closing out. Because sandbars constantly form and reform, channels may appear or disappear overnight. Beach breaks with multiple peaks can accommodate more surfers than other breaks.

locals

OUTSIDE

INSIDE

going right

going left

mushy waves

wave section

close out

River Mouth Breaks
The outflow of water from a river may shape the bottom sediments so they resemble a point break. River mouths can be notoriously sharky or have tricky currents, so check with locals first and have more than one bail-out point in mind.

and then subside in a deepwater channel so you can get off before they hit land. Spilling waves are the best waves for kayak surfing in general. Plunging or tubing waves can be good for experienced surfers in high-performance boats. Surging waves are more fun for playing in rock gardens than surfing. Avoid places where the waves break all at once (close out) or break directly on the beach (shore break).

Being choosy about your surf spot can make the difference between a fun surf frolic and a gear-scattering epic. Factor in the swell size and direction, wind speed and direction, the tide, the crowds, your experience, and equipment. Having said that, don't fall into the trap of wasting the entire day searching for the "perfect" wave. Never leave good surf.

Selecting Your Boat and Paddle

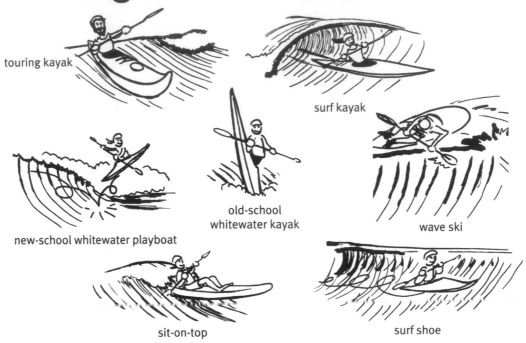

touring kayak

surf kayak

new-school whitewater playboat

old-school whitewater kayak

wave ski

sit-on-top

surf shoe

While classic touring kayaks catch waves easily and are capable of maneuvering in and out of the surf zone, they have displacement hulls that are designed to move through the water, not skim over it. Surfing in them is a bit like bombing down a mogul run with your touring skis or bunny hopping down a rocky trail with your road bike. You may have long rides on small spilling waves, but if the waves steepen you will want a shorter boat with a flat-bottomed planing hull that can skim across the surface at high speeds. You will have a lot more fun, be more in control, and be less of a liability to others. Hard rails or chines and fins help a surf kayak find traction across a steep wave face without sliding sideways and spinning out like a Frisbee. In general, good surf boats have low-volume sterns that slice under the foam of a broken wave. This feature enables you to ride straight toward the beach (front surf) and stay in control in the soup instead of broaching sideways and becoming a bulldozer.

International-class surf kayaks have long, flattened hulls enabling them to accelerate quickly. Wave skis are short sit-on-top surfboards that can perform well on steeper waves but, like surfboards, are not fast enough to catch waves with a shallow slope. Surf shoes look and act like a cross between surfboards and flying saucers. Old-school whitewater kayaks are great fun until you surf with someone in a surf kayak and see what they can do. Whitewater playboats, while painfully slow for catching waves, excel in maneuvers in the foam. Some sea kayakers carry or tow their playboats or surfboards on their touring kayaks to access secret spots.

Secure your rudder with a shock cord to keep it and anyone else from getting mangled. Always wear a helmet in the surf, even for sandy bottoms. A shorter paddle facilitates quick maneuvers and accelerations.

Catching Waves

Position yourself just offshore from the take-off zone or peak, where the waves break first. (You can also start at the shoulder, where it may be more mellow.) The faster your boat, the farther out you can be. Good wave selection can be critical, so learn to read which way and how hard waves are going to break.

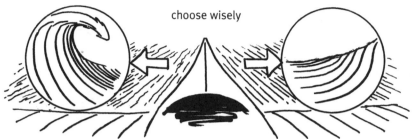

choose wisely

When you see a wave you want, paddle to intercept it at the steepest part. Catching a wave is more a matter of speed than leaning forward; sit upright so you can paddle faster. Match the speed of the wave as if you were in a relay race. The wave should catch up with you when the face is steep enough to slide down but before it breaks. Look left and right to see which way you want to go.

Adjust your angle depending on wave steepness. If you are at the peak early (A), paddle straight ahead to catch the wave and turn as the wave steepens. If you are at the peak late (B), angle in the direction you want to surf.

If you are on a gentle shoulder, the wave might not be steep enough to catch if you paddle straight or in the direction you want to surf (C). Angle your kayak toward the steeper section where it will break first to catch it (D) and then quickly turn where you want to go (E).

You have to *want* the wave. The later waves in the set are often the biggest and break farthest out. If you try to catch a wave and are not fully committed, you will miss it and be pummeled by the rest of the set.

Staying in Control

Good boat control lets you have fun, avoid hazards, and keep from being a hazard to others.

On the Wave Face

Once you catch a wave, turn your boat in the direction you want to go (usually toward the shoulder) before the wave breaks. It is easier to turn while your bow is in the air. Use a stern rudder stroke and follow it with a forward sweep on the opposite side to keep your speed. Once you turn, your kayak tends to keep turning up and over the crest of the wave, ending your ride. To exit more quickly, rudder on the wave side. To stay on the wave, rudder on the shoreward side, using your paddle blade as an adjustable surfboard fin.

The steeper the wave, the stronger a ruddering stroke you will need on the shore side to hold your line.

lean to the outside of the turn

bow free

no rudder

rudder

side surf

cut across face

right rudder

quick exit

cut back or turn toward shore

no rudder

exit

keep cutting across face

To go faster, angle your kayak across the steepest part of the face and lean forward. To slow down, rudder back up the wave face or place your boat on the flats in front of the wave.

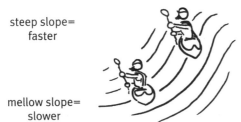

steep slope= faster

mellow slope= slower

wave steepness

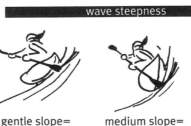

gentle slope= normal rudder

medium slope= deep rudder

steep slope= fins needed

In the Soup

Once the wave breaks around you and you are stuck in the foam, you can still maneuver to avoid obstacles or regain the green face of a wave.

To move forward, start with a low brace (1) and slice your blade edge forward through the foam pile (2), twisting your entire torso and winding up for the next stroke. Then dig your blade into the foam pile (3) and do a forward sweep (4). Repeat as needed to move yourself back and forth along the wave front.

To move backward, start with a high brace (1) and skim your blade backward through the pile (2). Dig your blade into the foam pile (3) and do a reverse sweep all the way to your toes (4). Repeat as needed.

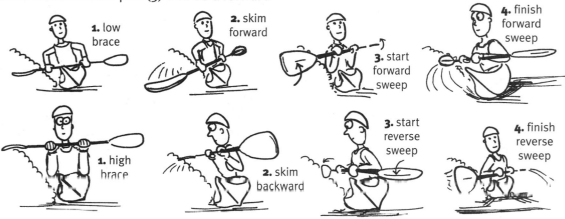

Spins with a Displacement Hull

When half of your kayak is being pushed to shore by the whitewater and the other half is being dragged over the back of the wave by the green water, this push and pull will spin your kayak around. You can control this spin by adjusting your kayak's position on the edge of the foam pile. Once you spin 90° and are facing the sea, you should have a neutral lean side to side. Once you spin past this point you will need to switch your lean to the other side because the whitewater will now be on your other side. For multiple spins, keep up with the edge of the pocket.

switch lean!

switch lean!

Flat Spins with a Planing Hull

Planing hulls with enough rocker will spin on the unbroken face of a wave once it is steep enough to reach planing speed. Initiate a spin by turning your head and cranking a reverse sweep in the direction you want to spin. The taller the wave, the more spins are possible. The greater challenge is making these spud boats go straight. Use bow or stern rudder strokes to stop or stave off your spins.

head turned over shoulder

reverse sweep

planing speed

Surfing Maneuvers

With experience you can tell whether the section of wave in front of you is going to jack up, mush out, or close out. The following list of moves will give you some ideas of what options you have. Once you are familiar with several maneuvers, you can start linking them together on the same wave.

Roller Coaster

A roller coaster is a series of turns up and down the face of a wave accomplished by ruddering on opposite sides. In addition to being fun, this is a good way to dodge other surfers.

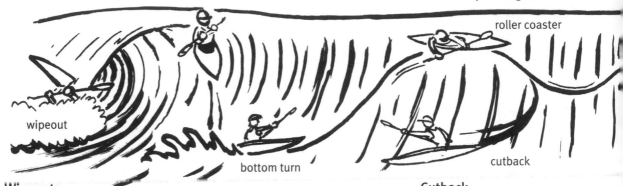

wipeout

roller coaster

bottom turn

cutback

Wipeouts

Wipeouts are one of the most important moves. Most new surfing maneuvers were born from magnificent wipeouts that were later refined as folks replicated them on purpose. The most memorable wipeouts involve going "over the falls" with the descending lip of a tubing wave. When you wipe out, go big and wipe out with style.

Bottom Turn

A bottom turn is a dramatic carve to avoid being crushed by the lip after you drop down the face of a steep wave. Initiate it with a stern rudder and follow with a boat lean into the turn.

Cutback

A cutback is a dramatic change of direction on the wave face. You can cut back toward the curl if you have surfed too far along the face and want to turn around again. Roundhouse cutbacks utilize the breaking part of the wave to move your bow around.

Tube Rides

While aerial blunts and kick flips are pretty hip right now, getting tubed will always be the ultimate in cool. Wave selection, kayak placement, and timing are all crucial. Choose a wave that will actually tube, and position your kayak on the wave face where you predict the tube will form. If you're too high you'll kick out or do a floater and if you're too low you'll get creamed by the lip. Adjust your speed so the lip overtakes without burying you too deeply. Whatever happens, it will be cool.

lining up under or behind peak

tube ride

WHOOMPH!

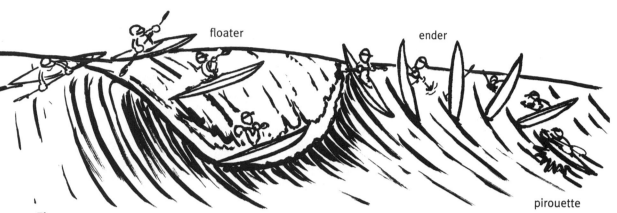

floater

ender

pirouette

Floater

A floater is when you place yourself on the lip of a wave as it breaks so you "float" down the foam pile and land in front of the wave. This is a fun move on close-out sections but it usually resigns you to surfing all the way to shore.

Ender

An ender is a vertical move when your bow pearls or dives just as the wave breaks and pitches your stern over you. You will then land upside down so remember to tuck your head. A well-timed reverse sweep can turn a normal ender into a pirouette.

Backsurfing and Backenders

In addition to being an integral part of spins, backsurfing is tremendously fun in its own right. You get amazing views of the wave you might not normally see, but need to be particularly aware of other surfers around you. Use a bow rudder (and a cross-bow rudder for quick responses) to steer. Start by paddling backward and steering with a bow rudder or reverse sweeps, or by front surfing and spinning. A backender is simply a backward ender, usually the result of a steep backsurf or an encounter with a particularly formidable wave when paddling back out.

bow rudder

bow rudder

bow rudder

backsurf

backender

Cartwheels

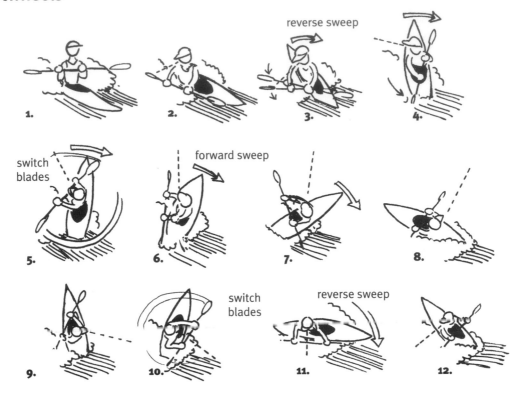

Cartwheels are a series of propeller-style spins with one end of the boat buried in the water at a time. Cartwheels are most easily performed in a very short kayak or one with a potato-chip-thin bow and stern that slice through the water while your kayak is on edge in the foam. The key to this maneuver is leaning your kayak far enough on edge, looking where you want your bow to go, and sweeping your lower blade from your bow to your stern or vice versa. There are entire chapters devoted to this maneuver in other texts, but these are the basic steps:

1. Begin by front surfing in the foam. 2–4. Lean your boat on edge and bury the bow with a reverse sweep that lifts the stern. When your stern goes up in the air and your reverse sweep reaches the bow, look over your shoulder in the direction you want your bow to go. 5–7. While up in the air, wind up your torso and place your other blade at the bow and begin a forward sweep to maintain the boat's momentum. 8–9. You now want your stern to slice underwater and your bow to come up. Again, lead with your head. 10–12. With your stern buried and your bow arcing shoreward, wind up your torso again and plant another reverse sweep just before your bow slices down again. Repeat as needed.

Blunts

Blunts are a 180° spin done at a slight angle so your stern clears the water like a low-angle cartwheel. They can be done either on the green or in the foam. Time your blunt for when you hit a bump on the wave face for an aerial experience. Build up speed and aim for a little rise to help lift your stern. Begin by looking where you want your bow to go; follow through with a reverse sweep and a subtle lean into the turn. The bow should slice underwater, allowing the stern to snap through the air and land flat into a back-surf.

Exiting the Wave

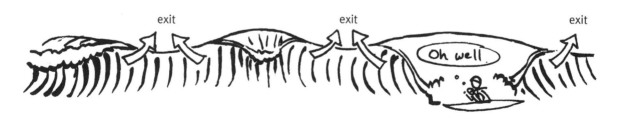

The easiest way to exit a wave is to kick out before it breaks. Change your lean back to neutral as you exit. If you wait until the wave breaks over you, you can sometimes make it through the wave with a strong reverse sweep. Once a wave has broken and you're in the middle of the foam, you may as well resign yourself to a long paddle back out. Occasionally some deep paddle strokes into the foam will bring you up and out the backside. Endering out, backendering out, or just flipping over will sometimes bring you out the back side as well.

Maneuvers When Paddling Back Out ⌐

Paddling back outside doesn't always have to be a grueling sprint. Take advantage of other opportunities to have fun and improve your boating skills.

Stern Squirts

Stern squirts are backenders with pirouettes done in kayaks with low-volume sterns as you paddle back out. Paddle toward the oncoming foam at a slight angle. Just before the foam hits the side of your bow, do a stern pry on the wave side to turn your boat into the wave. Tilt your boat away from your pry so your thin stern slices underwater. The whitewater will catch the underside of your bow and lift it up into the air as your kayak spins 180° on its axis so you land facing the shore (ideally). Usually you just end up upside down in the soup.

Lip Turn

This is one instance where kayaks have an advantage over surfboards. A lip turn is when you catch a wave as you paddle back out. Paddle at an angle toward the pocket of a peeling breaker. As the front half of your kayak is pushed around by the foam pile, lean into the turn and pivot your boat with a forward or reverse sweep, just like a roundhouse cutback.

Wave Wheels

Wave wheels are cartwheels done while paddling out over the top of a wave with the help of the wave crest and trough. Paddle up the face of the wave with your normal sense of expediency. Just before you reach the crest, tilt your kayak on edge and do a forward sweep on the side you leaned into the wave to sink your stern in the wave face. As the wave crest passes beneath your bow, switch your forward sweep into a reverse sweep and drive your bow through the air over the crest. Because the wave has passed beneath you, you are now in the air where your kayak is free to continue to rotate. Ideally, your boat should cartwheel in the air so you land stern-first in the trough or continue cartwheeling.

Kick Flips

I'm going to do one of these one day, honestly. Kick flips are Eskimo rolls done in the air as your kayak launches off the back of a wave. You need a big, steep wave that is just about to break and an oh-so-cool solid back deck roll. As you launch over the crest, hurl yourself over with enough momentum to roll the kayak upside down and around, where you land on a brace.

Surfing Etiquette

or Why Board Surfers Dislike Kayakers

Waves in prime surfing areas are a limited resource and locals there inevitably become protective and territorial. Surfers don't even like each other, much less us butt-surfers. Wave rage, harsh words, and ice-picked kayaks can occur in crowded places.

To compound this issue, many early kayak surfers were completely clueless about surf etiquette and safety. They hogged waves, surfed out of control, ran over surfers, and then wondered why nobody liked them. Now kayakers have an unfortunate reputation and have a long way to go to earn the trust and respect of board surfers. Some surfers will always be rude, but I have found most to be accepting if you follow a few simple rules, control your boat, and act generously in the lineup.

The Lineup

The best surfers occupy the best spot and claim the best waves, leaving the mediocre waves for the less able surfers and newcomers to fight over. After one surfer catches a wave, the other surfers jockey for position on the next wave. While not necessarily egalitarian, this is the protocol. Start by sitting off to the side so you can observe the hierarchy and the rotation within the pack. Be content with leftovers to start with, and move up the food chain as appropriate.

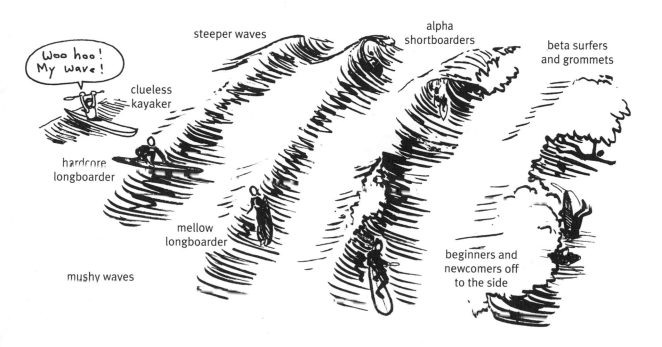

Woo hoo! My wave!

clueless kayaker

steeper waves

alpha shortboarders

beta surfers and grommets

hardcore longboarder

mellow longboarder

mushy waves

beginners and newcomers off to the side

Take-Off Points

Because of their faster paddling speed and longer length, kayaks can usually catch waves farther out than surfboards. Because the first person on the wave usually has the right of way, kayakers can quickly take over a place and hog the best waves. If you do take the position farthest out, show some restraint. Board surfers will be amazed.

Determining the Right of Way and Dropping In

The first person gliding freely on a wave has the right of way. If two surfers catch a wave at the same time, the person closest to the curl has the right of way. If you "drop in" in front of a surfer already on the wave, you not only ruin the wave for that surfer but also create a hazard. Because experienced surfers travel across the face of the wave and beginners tend to surf straight toward shore, you can see why beginners should choose their waves carefully.

If the person kicks out, wipes out, gets closed out, or goes the other direction, the wave is then open. If someone drops in on you, a brief attention-getting sound should alert her to your presence and she should kick out. If people keep dropping in on you, avoid inflammatory language and actions, as this behavior never improves the situation. Work it out, paddle over to a different break, or come back later.

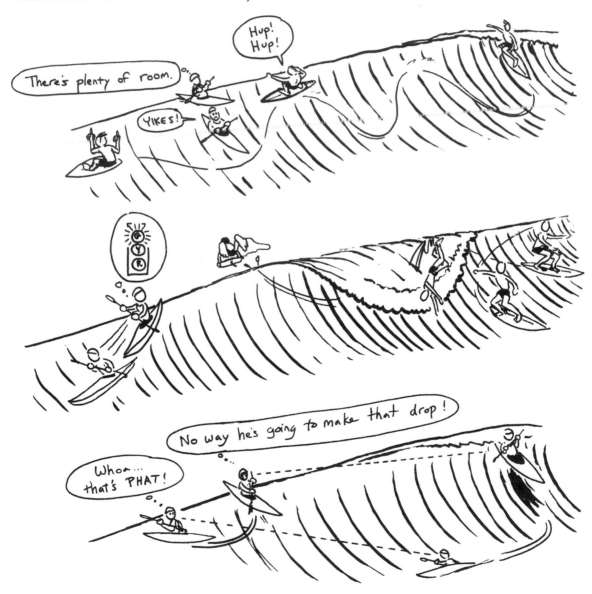

If you are unsure if a surfer is going to wipe-out or make a section, you can start down the wave as long as you leave enough space to pull out if they do make the section.

Since lightweight surfboards can accelerate much faster than kayaks, give them more room than you think they need. Never assume that a surfer is not there just because you cannot see her.

Snaking a wave is catching a wave behind the first person on a wave and will get you in trouble if the surfer decides to cut back.

Paddling Back Out

When paddling back out it can be hard to see what's coming beyond the next wave. Gain a few seconds of advanced warning by reading other surfers' faces, and act accordingly.

Paddle back out in the channel to avoid other surfers. If you are paddling back out and someone is surfing toward you, yield to the person on the wave so they can stay in the pocket. Surfers on a clean face can generally maneuver around you if they have a good idea of where you are going and you don't change your mind. If it looks like it's going to be close, abandon your sprint for the shoulder and resign yourself to getting slammed by the soup. If you are on a collision course with someone else and can't get out of the way, flip over so they hit your hull instead of your head.

Surfing is an ever-evolving sport, but the fundamental sense of wonder remains at the core. You can be just as stoked riding a ripple all the way to the beach as nailing that aerial blunt. Remember the most important thing about surfing is simply being stoked to be out there.

surfer's view

Reefs and Rocks

When you paddle along an exposed coast-line, you realize that you are in a very small boat on a very big ocean next to a very solid continent. This realm of rocks and reefs is one of the most dynamic regions on the planet. Waves sculpt mountainsides into terraces, arches, sea stacks, and reefs while tectonic forces raise the seabed back up again. If not for the uplift of new moun-tain ranges, the continent would be whittled away to a sandbar in less than 20 million years. If the conditions are right and your skills and experience are up for it, you can find a dynamic playground of fantastic features. Preparation for paddling here includes comfort and control in the surf zone, a bomber roll, a helmet, float bags, and an intimate knowledge of rescue options. The best way to ex-

> *"They are wet with the showers of mountains, and embrace the rock for want of shelter."*
> —JOB 24:8

plore the open coast for the first several times is with a class or a group of seasoned paddles familiar with the area.

The most famous group that has pushed the coastal kayaking envelope is the Tsunami Rangers of Northern California. These wave warriors specialize in spectacular stunts including surfing though sea caves. *Extreme Sea Kayaking* by Eric Soares and Michael Powers is the best source of information and attitude for paddling in this dynamic area. John Lull's *Sea Kayaking Safety and Rescue* is another excellent reference for rock garden paddling.

Where and When to Go

The best time to explore the open coast is when you're bored because the waves are too small for your favorite surf break. In a decent swell, access into, out of, and along rock gardens can be severely limited by offshore breakers. Even storm chop on a lake can transform a formerly placid rocky lake shoreline into a potentially dangerous impact zone. Boomers are submerged rocks that waves break on unexpectedly as the tide drops or when a particularly large set comes. Small conditions make rock gardens more interesting, inviting, and intimate. Keep an eye out for basking seals and sea lions and give them a wide berth before they give you a "heads-up" and stampede into the sea (see the Special Topics chapter).

Midtide is usually the best time to take advantage of rock garden features. At high tide a lot of outcrops and sea caves are submerged, while at low tide you may not have enough water to paddle over and around rocks. Note the type of waves. Are they spilling, surging, or plunging? Rock gardens are where surging waves come into their own and make a place more interesting. Remember that the waves are always bigger when you're out there.

The best way to assess where you want to go and don't want to go is to watch and wait for fifteen minutes or more for the largest waves to come. Big waves act like radar blips and can tell you what the underwater topography is like and where the safety and danger zones are.

Rock Garden Anatomy ～

Safety Zones

Safety zones are the equivalent of eddies on a river. You can relax, hang out, and catch your breath, but may have to use good boat control to stay there. Safety zones are either channels too deep for waves to break or wave shadows behind large rocks that block incoming surf. You might have surges and swirls here, but the whitewater is limited to a size you can easily paddle through. If you are stressed out or in danger there, it isn't a safety zone.

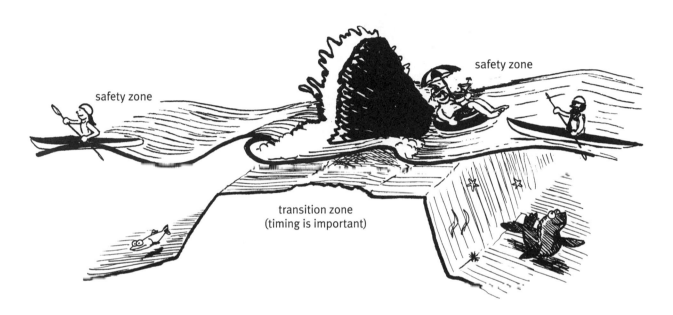

safety zone

safety zone

transition zone
(timing is important)

Transition Zones

Transition zones are like busy streets or packed shipping lanes with waves taking the place of traffic. There are times to cross and times when you don't want to be near the place. The challenge is learning to read the waves to tell the difference. An example of a transition zone is a shallow reef that you can paddle across between sets but that turns into an impact zone when a wave comes.

Seal Launching and Landing

he who hesitates   just right   jumping the gun

1.

2.

When you don't have the luxury of a nice harbor mouth or sandy beach with gentle surf, launching from a rock can be an option. Place your kayak on a nonstick rock or convenient pile of seaweed and wait for a wave. When a wave comes, wait until the shoreward rush has slowed down enough so you won't be swept backward. If you launch too soon, you will land on rocks and then be swept backward into your launching pad. If you launch too late, you will be stranded in the impact zone. A trusted friend can help push you off, but make sure that you agree on a launch signal and that your friend has easy access to high ground.

If you have a small surf kayak you can jump into the water with it, paddle it away from the shore break like a surfboard, and climb in it. If you have a larger kayak you can toss your boat in first and then swim after it. Make sure you don't lose track of your boat when you do this.

Yahoo - yak - bo - doo!

To land in rock gardens, go in small conditions, use extreme caution, and examine all your options. Use a sandy beach if available and appropriate. If the area is protected enough, you can also sideslip over to a convenient rock, hop out, and pull your kayak up behind you.

To make a seal landing on top of a rock, carefully select a flat, protected landing spot in the surge range. Time your approach to ride in on top of a surging wave so you have a cushion to coast over. Land straight, as described on page 142, and make a quick exit before the next set comes.

Places You Don't Want to Be

(and what to do if you end up there)

When transition zones turn bad, you can end up in a danger zone. Generally you know when this has happened. Here are some tips on what to do next.

A. Down-wave of kayak in the surf or in a potential surf zone. Being directly behind someone punching through a wave is an accident waiting to happen. Move to the side or flip upside down if a collision with another kayaker seems unavoidable.

B. Between a wave and a hard place. If you find yourself between a breaking wave and a rock, don't become caught in the headlights. Paddle really fast, tuck, and come up paddling.

C. Sidesurfing toward rocks. If you are sidesurfing toward rocks and can't get off the wave, paddle forward or backward to steer toward a deeper channel or the "softest" spot. If that doesn't work, don't give up. Flip over into the wave to slow yourself down so the wave passes over you, and then roll back up.

D. Surfing into a rock. If you are going to hit a rock, lean into the wave so you hit the rocks with your hull instead of your head. I like to lean forward to help my torso absorb the impact.

E. Stuck on top of a rock. If you find yourself stuck up on top of a rock, smile and act like you meant to be there. Pivot your kayak to face the next wave for a smooth seal launch or exit your boat quickly and move to a safer spot.

F. Stuck in a hydraulic. Hydraulics form when water rushes over a rock and recirculates like a vertical eddy. Unlike in rivers, rock garden hydraulics appear and disappear as the water surges in and out. Treat them like breaking waves and punch straight through them. If you become caught in one, tilt your boat "downstream" (the direction changes with the surge) until the hydraulic disappears or paddle out the side.

G. Upside down in the mosh pit. When upside down in the rocks or against a cliff, tuck and make your roll a good one. If you miss a roll, try rolling up on the other side.

H. Swimming among the rocks. If you swim in the rocks, don't get between your kayak and a hard place. Swim toward a safety zone (inside or outside) where you can reseat yourself with an appropriate rescue. Tow your kayak or push it in front of you. If someone offers you a tow, try to hold onto your boat and paddle and help by kicking.

catching a
wave in

riding wave in, feet
first in the shallows

high ground
safety zone

I.

riding undertow
out to deepwater
safety zone

I. Stranded when a monster wave comes. If a monster wave comes and you can't clamber to higher ground, play barnacle and cling to the backside of a rock, keeping a low profile. If a wave pries you off, tuck into a ball or go limp. Once you regain a grip, swim, run, or crawl into a safety zone. To reach shore, swim aggressively and then ride the surge behind breaking waves with your feet up to fend off rocks. To reach deeper water, use the outgoing undertow and dive under waves.

Fun Stuff to Do

Paddlers don't just go to these places to get trashed, scared, and demoralized. The ability to negotiate rock gardens opens up enormous stretches of inaccessible coastline and remote surf breaks. Some unique play situations form that you can take advantage of in the right conditions if you know what to look for and what to avoid.

deep ↓

↑ shallow

Paddling Next to Rocks

Where the waves are surging, you can paddle right next to rocks and glide right past them. Avoid shallow places where the waves will change from surging to spilling or plunging. Be ready to punch out through a breaking wave or deal with a rock should you find yourself pushed into it.

Hiding Behind Rocks

In addition to being an important maneuver in rock gardens, hiding behind rocks can be incredibly exciting. Tucking behind a rock as a large set slams in is like being in a cave behind a waterfall. Foam showers and bouncing surge transform your boat into a bathtub toy. Your rock should be large enough to shield you from the largest sets. These safety zones may be very small, so be sure to have good boat control in all directions. Be aware of undercut rocks that currents can suck you under or that a rising surge can wedge your boat underneath.

Paddling over Rocks

Paddling in between and over rocks is a great test of your timing, skill, and intelligence. The idea is to paddle across a shallow spot when a wave increases the water depth. Stay on top of the wave where the water is deep enough to clear the obstacle. Catch enough of the wave's momentum to coast over the obstacle on a cushion of water without sliding ahead of the wave where you can quickly run out of water. When done correctly, you feel like you're riding a flying carpet. Watch and wait for patterns, as timing is crucial. Start with submerged rocks and tiny waves. Watch which direction the current goes and go with the flow. Have a Plan B for when you get stuck.

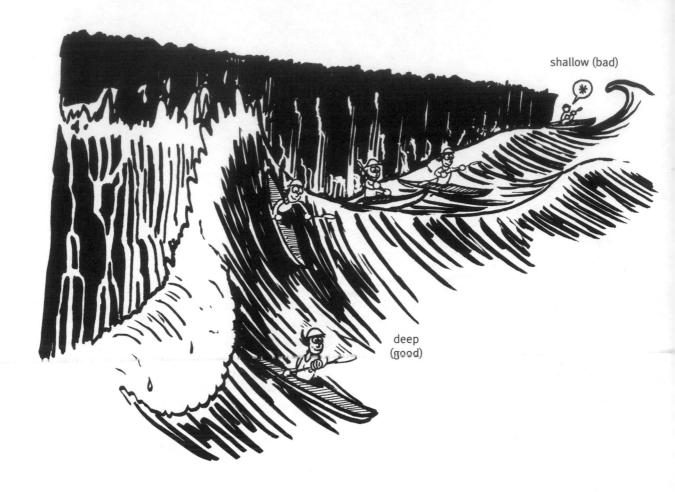

shallow (bad)

deep
(good)

Surfing Reactionary Waves to Sea

When surging waves hit a steep shoreline, they often bounce back to sea and can be surfed for a short distance. Wait and watch the area from a safe distance to make sure the largest waves don't break before reaching the cliff. Set up facing seaward with your stern two to three feet from the cliff (watch your stern!). When the wave comes, your stern will rise up, you will get showered with a huge splash, then your boat will accelerate seaward, driven by the backwash.

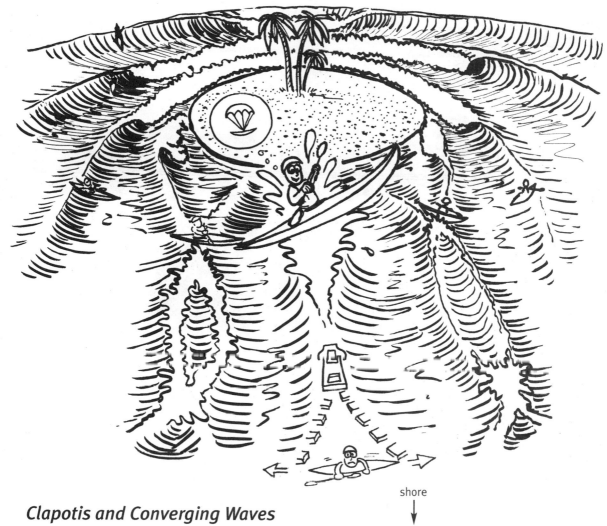

shore ↓

Clapotis and Converging Waves

When two waves from opposite directions collide, they pass through each other with spectacular results, similar to a volcano erupting. Waves that hit at an angle create a giant zippering effect. The chaos formed from reactionary and incoming waves is known as clapotis and resembles being at the epicenter of an earthquake. Waves can also wrap around small islands to create this trampoline-like effect. In this circumstance, waves wash back and forth parallel to shore instead of taking you closer to shore.

Surfing converging waves converts your kayak into a giant skipping stone. Beware of hard landings and spinal compression. Map out safety zones and escape routes before attempting to surf in these situations.

incoming wave

clapotis

backwash from cliff

Sea Caves

Sea caves can be incredibly beautiful places to be as well as incredibly stupid places to be, depending on the conditions and the paddlers. Assess the hazard by watching and waiting for the largest sets of the day. A big surf day is not the day to go into a sea cave. Choose the flattest day of the year to check out that sea cave you've always wanted to explore. Avoid caves with sea water dripping from the ceiling. Ideally, visit during a falling tide rather than a rising tide. Before you explore a cave, post wave watchers at the mouth. They should be experienced paddlers who can judge a potentially dangerous wave and warn you of its approach.

Backing into a cave gives you more options than paddling in forward. You can see what waves are coming, quickly exit the cave if needed, and power straight through a breaking wave if necessary. Go in one paddler at a time. Move around obstacles as you rise and fall with the surge. Once you are in a sea cave, locate the highest part of the ceiling and any rocks or features that you can hide behind if a wave comes. Waterproof flashlights can be helpful in deep caves. Currents in sea caves can be fast and unpredictable, particularly at the intersection of several passages.

To negotiate narrow passages, build momentum and use your hands to guide yourself through. Time your passage to coincide with

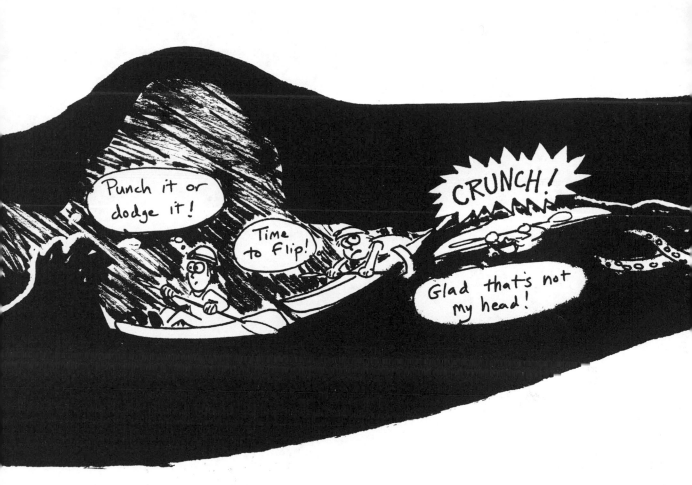

the currents moving in the same direction. Take care to keep your kayak from becoming wedged sideways in a passage.

If an attention-getting wave comes, you have several options. Exit the cave quickly for deeper water, build up speed to punch through the wave, or hide behind a rock (watch out for the wave reflection). If the wave has not broken, position yourself under a high point in the ceiling. Be aware that this will probably be the first of several waves. If you think you could hit the ceiling, flip over and roll up afterward. Not only is your hull harder than your head, but the buoyancy of your kayak beneath you can crush you against the ceiling. If this maneuver sounds daunting, perhaps you should not be there.

Regarding specific hazards, YOU'RE IN A SEA CAVE! It's all hazardous! Rescues are more dangerous, swimming is more dangerous, help from others is very difficult and unlikely. Ask yourself if you would be willing to swim and tow your kayak out of the cave to deeper water.

The bug-eyed paddlers and monster waves of this chapter are not intended to dissuade paddlers from trying these maneuvers. Try your luck in tiny conditions with 6" surges and low consequences. The most important thing is to have fun out there.

Tides and Currents

"The current and the tide rarely coincide."
—MARCÍ WISE

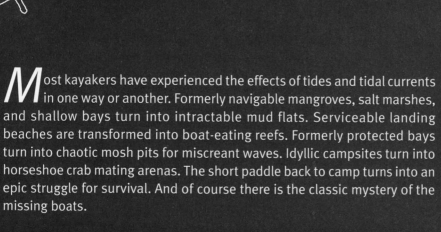

Most kayakers have experienced the effects of tides and tidal currents in one way or another. Formerly navigable mangroves, salt marshes, and shallow bays turn into intractable mud flats. Serviceable landing beaches are transformed into boat-eating reefs. Formerly protected bays turn into chaotic mosh pits for miscreant waves. Idyllic campsites turn into horseshoe crab mating arenas. The short paddle back to camp turns into an epic struggle for survival. And of course there is the classic mystery of the missing boats.

Ups and Downs ~

The earth, moon, and sun are in a three-way tug of war with each other for the earth's oceans. Because the earth is the closest body to the oceans, it has the strongest gravitational force and keeps the oceans firmly rooted in their basins for the most part. The moon has the next greatest influence on our seas because of its proximity, followed by the much more massive but much more distant sun. In large contiguous waterways, water "flows upward" in a bulge toward the moon (high tide) and away from areas with less lunar influence (low tide).

The earth and moon also spin around each other like square-dancing partners. Just as your hair sticks out behind you when you swing your partner round and round, the earth's oceans mass behind its central spinning point with the moon (another high tide).

Combine these opposing gravitational and centrifugal forces and you have the tides. The high tide bulges stay in place underneath and opposite the moon while the earth spins around underneath them. The sections of the oceans between the bulges provide the water for the bulges and experience low tides. When the moon is not directly above the equator, it pulls water unequally from the northern and southern hemispheres, creating subsequent high and low tides of different heights.

Let's pretend you are camping on an island in the bulge away from the moon and it is 12:00 noon. Six hours and twelve minutes later your island spins 90° relative to the moon and experiences low tide. At 12:25 AM your beach passes directly underneath the moon and it is high tide once again, and at 6:38 AM it is low tide again. At 12:50 the next day you are back in the centrifugal bulge. The ever-increasing time difference is due to the moon's own 28-day orbit around the earth, moving 50 minutes or 12.5° eastward each day. To figure out what tide it is, put down your calculator, pick up your tide table, and turn the page.

The sun can either enhance or diminish the moon's influence, depending on their relative positions to the earth, evident by the phase of

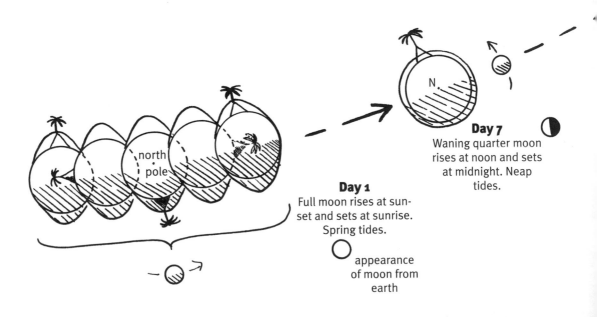

north pole

Day 1
Full moon rises at sunset and sets at sunrise. Spring tides.

appearance of moon from earth

Day 7
Waning quarter moon rises at noon and sets at midnight. Neap tides.

the moon. High amplitude or spring tides result every two weeks when the moon and sun line up during a full or new moon. When the moon and sun are at 90° during the intervening weeks, their gravitational forces are at odds with each other and result in minimal tidal ranges, or neap tides. Variations in the orbits of the moon and sun, ocean and shoreline geography, atmospheric pressure, friction, wind, rivers, and other factors affect the tidal range and current strength.

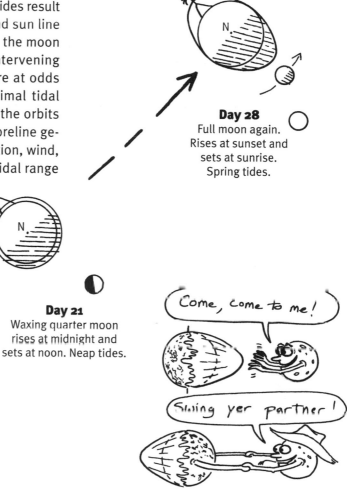

Day 28
Full moon again.
Rises at sunset and
sets at sunrise.
Spring tides.

Day 21
Waxing quarter moon
rises at midnight and
sets at noon. Neap tides.

Day 14
New moon rises at sunrise and sets at sunset.
Spring tides.

The moon pulls the ocean toward it
on the near side and flings it away
on the far side.

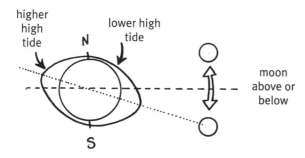

higher
high
tide
lower high
tide
N
S
moon
above or
below

What Tide it Is?

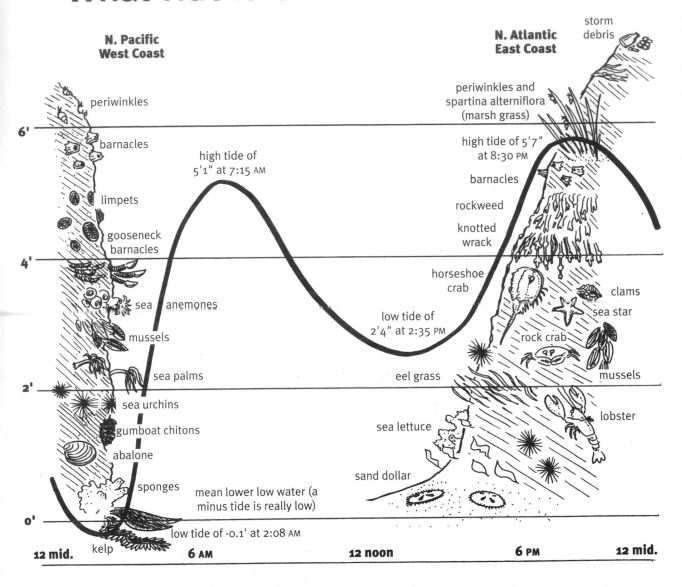

N. Pacific West Coast

N. Atlantic East Coast

storm debris

periwinkles

periwinkles and spartina alterniflora (marsh grass)

barnacles

high tide of 5'1" at 7:15 AM

high tide of 5'7" at 8:30 PM

barnacles

rockweed

limpets

knotted wrack

gooseneck barnacles

horseshoe crab

clams

sea star

sea anemones

low tide of 2'4" at 2:35 PM

rock crab

mussels

mussels

sea palms

eel grass

sea urchins

lobster

gumboat chitons

sea lettuce

abalone

sponges

mean lower low water (a minus tide is really low)

sand dollar

kelp

low tide of -0.1' at 2:08 AM

12 mid.   6 AM   12 noon   6 PM   12 mid.

Tides are measured from the mean lower low water level (MLLW on charts). Tide ranges vary from negligible to a towering 40+ feet where amplified by basin geography. Most oceans slosh back and forth twice a day, producing two high and two low tides each day. In other places, the moon has a much smaller effect and the tides are based only on the sun and rise every 24 hours instead of 12.

If you forget your tide table on your kitchen table, you can gain a sense of what tide it is from what critters and debris are exposed and then extrapolate the next high and low tide. The wrack line is a line of debris washed ashore from previous high tides. Piles of logs, bits of Styrofoam, and plastic bottles behind dunes show old storm surge levels.

How Tides Make Currents ～

Tides and Currents Aligned

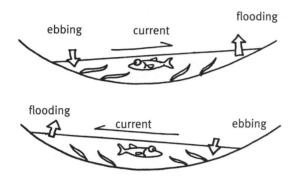 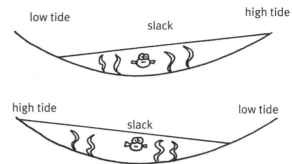

Water flows from connected waterways to gather underneath and opposite the moon at high tide. When this bulge is forced through narrow passages, significant currents can occur. Think back to the rubber ducky sloshing back and forth in your bathtub. Currents flood inland at midtide as the water rushes upward, pause at the moment of high tide, reverse as the water drains away and pause again at low tide.

Tides and Currents Not Aligned

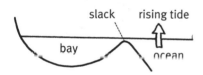 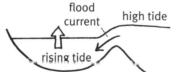 

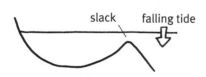 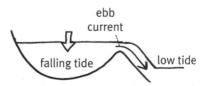 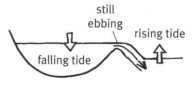

In many cases, however, the current and tide are not so neatly aligned. As the tide rises and starts to spill through a restricted passage into an enclosed bay, it creates a flood current. Even after high tide is reached at the constriction, the current will continue to flow into the bay because the ocean level is still higher than the bay level. Slack tide occurs only when the ocean level drops down to where it matches the water level in the bay. As the ocean continues to drop below the bay level, the water flows outward as an ebb current. This flow continues even past low tide until the ocean level rises to meet it once again at a slack tide. Unlike the bathtub example, maximum flows are found during high and low tides.

Other Current Events

Eddies and Eddylines

Where the current meets islands, points, reefs, or bridge pilings, it goes around these obstructions and leaves a void behind them. Water farther downstream flows back to fill in this neglected space, creating an upstream current or an eddy. An eddyline is like an earthquake fault dividing these two masses moving in opposite directions. The upstream end of an eddyline tends to be narrow and distinct and can be a good place to cross if you are ready for fast and dynamic turns. Farther downstream the eddyline becomes more chaotic and unpredictable, characterized by boils, surges, seams

of converging currents, and whirlpools. Eventually the eddyline weakens and dissipates as you travel downstream. Minimize the time you spend in the turbulence by crossing eddylines at the far upstream end, where they are strong but narrow, or well downstream below the boils where they are wider and weaker. See the next chapter on River Touring for specific tips on boat leans and strokes for eddy turns and peel-outs. If you need to make headway against a current, take advantage of available eddies for an upstream ride.

Wind and Waves

When incoming waves run against or with a current, they slow down and bunch together or speed up and spread out, respectively. When incoming waves meet an outgoing current, it is like a line of people going up an escalator the wrong way. As the wavelengths become shorter, the waves become steeper and possibly break. When waves and currents go in the same direction the wavelength is stretched out, lowering the angle of the wave slopes and smoothing the seas. Because winds create waves, use tide tables and weather forecasts to avoid being in the midst of opposing winds and currents.

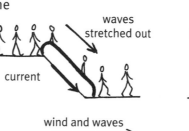

waves stretched out

current

waves bunched up

current

wind and waves

current

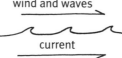

wind and waves

current

Tidal Bores

A tidal bore occurs when a rising tide is funneled into a narrow inlet or river mouth. As the funnel narrows and the depth decreases, a wedge of water is formed that moves upstream. This wave can steepen and break under the right conditions. While certain tidal bores may be fun for experts in a playboat, many constitute a very serious navigational hazard. Obtain expert local knowledge before paddling in these areas.

Are there tides here in the Bay of Fundy?

Yeah, but I hear they're a bore.

tidal bore

Tide Rips

Tide rips are rapids created by tidal currents in constricted or obstructed channels. Although some are to be avoided, others create fantastic play spots for skilled paddlers. Wear a helmet, know the area, and have a rescue plan so everyone knows what to do and where to go in case of a swim.

tide rip

Using Tides and Currents to Your Advantage

Why is this so hard?

To sea kayakers, tidal currents are the BART, METRO, or the T, tide tables are the daily schedule, and current charts are the route lines. If you are tide-smart, you can go anywhere with a minimum of effort on the lunar express. Misjudging the tide can be like arriving at a seedy bus station at 2 AM. Time your paddling routes to take advantage of the most favorable tides. Launching and landing at high tide can shorten the distance for carrying boats and gear, while low tide can protect a beach from offshore breakers. Be aware that a change in water level is much more significant in a shallow bay than on a deep cliff. Aside from the obvious concern of getting stuck, very shallow water slows your kayak down.

Which Way Does the Tide Go?

When you are in the middle of a crossing, it can be hard to tell if the current is helping or hurting you. Watch buoys, kelp, flotsam, and other boats to see which way they are moving. Ripples form more easily when the wind opposes the current, leaving glassy areas where the wind and currents are in line with each other. In addition to using ranges to see if you are staying on course, set up ranges to your side to make sure you are actually making progress toward your goal.

smooth: wind and currents aligned

choppy: wind and currents opposing

Coping with Currents

Ferries

To cross a current without losing ground, angle your kayak upstream. The faster the current, the more you have to head upstream (up to a point, or you go nowhere!). Be mindful that the speed and direction of the currents change as you cross. Monitor your progress and adjust your speed and angle to reach your goal with the least amount of work.

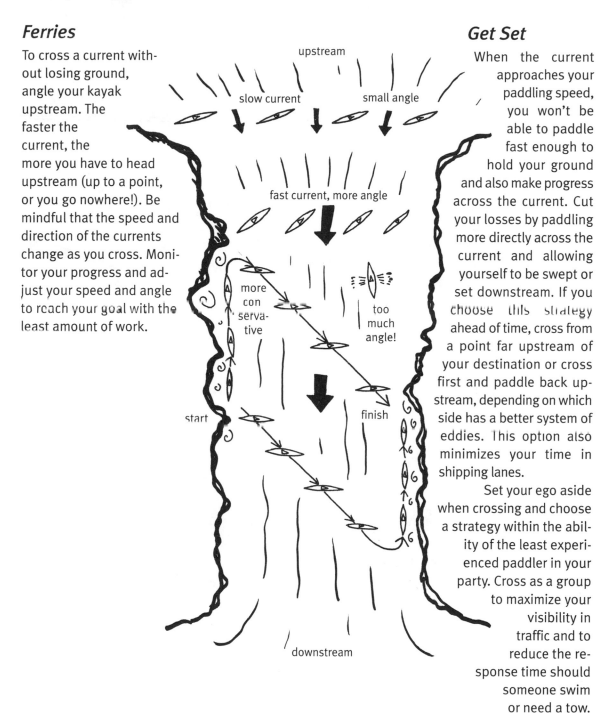

upstream

slow current

small angle

fast current, more angle

more conservative

too much angle!

start

finish

downstream

Get Set

When the current approaches your paddling speed, you won't be able to paddle fast enough to hold your ground and also make progress across the current. Cut your losses by paddling more directly across the current and allowing yourself to be swept or set downstream. If you choose this strategy ahead of time, cross from a point far upstream of your destination or cross first and paddle back upstream, depending on which side has a better system of eddies. This option also minimizes your time in shipping lanes.

Set your ego aside when crossing and choose a strategy within the ability of the least experienced paddler in your party. Cross as a group to maximize your visibility in traffic and to reduce the response time should someone swim or need a tow.

River Touring

"By such a river it is impossible to believe that one will ever be tired or old."
— WALLACE STEGNER, THE SOUND OF MOUNTAIN WATER

Just because you paddle a sea kayak doesn't mean you can't paddle it on a river. Paddling down an easy river is just like riding a perpetually ebbing tide. Because recreational and touring kayaks are not as maneuverable as river kayaks, you should limit your paddling to straightforward rivers that don't require quick turns and are rated class II or less (on a scale of I to VI). When you're upside down in moving water, the rocks come to you, so you should use a helmet if you paddle a closed-deck boat. Be certain to have inflated airbags and stash all ropes and lines to prevent entanglement in case of a swim.

If you are itching to take on anything bigger than class II, take a whitewater course and use a more maneuverable river kayak. There are also many excellent whitewater books available, such as William Nealy's classic, *Kayak*.

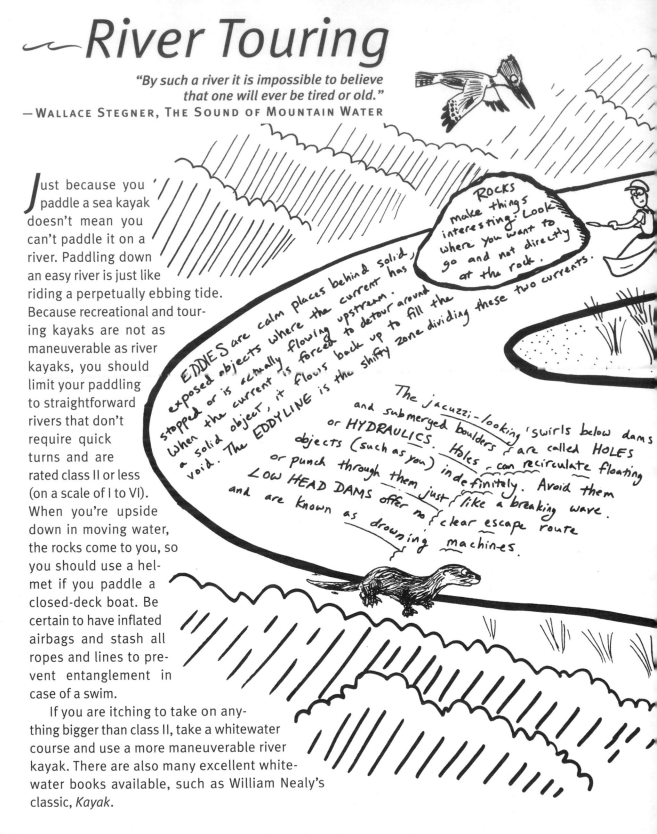

ROCKS make things interesting. Look where you want to go and not directly at the rock.

EDDIES are calm places behind solid, exposed objects where the current has stopped or is actually flowing upstream. When the current is forced to detour around a solid object, it flows back up to fill the void. The EDDYLINE is the shifty zone dividing these two currents.

The jacuzzi-looking swirls below dams and submerged boulders are called HOLES or HYDRAULICS. Holes can recirculate floating objects (such as you) indefinitely. Avoid them or punch through them just like a breaking wave. LOW HEAD DAMS offer no clear escape route and are known as drowning machines.

READING WATER is the art of interpreting underwater topography and knowing where to go from watching the surface of the water.

WAVE TRAIN is a series of standing waves marking a deep channel. These are generally fun places to be as long as the run-out downstream is clear. The same techniques for punching through and surfing ocean waves apply to river waves.

When discussing where to go with your partner, keep in mind that the directions **RIVER LEFT** and **RIVER RIGHT** are given from the perspective of someone facing downstream, regardless of which way someone is actually facing.

BENDS are a river's way of exploring. As a river bends to one side, the current shoots straight ahead and ricochets off the outside of the bend. This fast water scours out a deeper channel but also undermines the bank. The outside of a bend is like the Dark Side of the Force: once you start down that path, forever will it dominate your destiny. The inside of the bend is slower and shallower. By paddling down the inside of a bend, you keep all your options open and can easily go back to the deeper water on the outside if the channel is clear.

STRAINERS are downed trees or other obstacles that allow water to flow through them but trap solid objects (such as you). Always give them a wide berth.

Flipping and Swimming

Most swims occur on class II water where there is enough force to flip boats over but the rapids don't look dangerous enough to dissuade beginners from attempting it. If you flip upside down on a river, tuck and wet exit the same way as in the ocean.

If you are about to hit a rock or any other obstacle that can stop your boat, lean your boat into it so the moving water hits the bottom of your boat. Next, push yourself off to either side with your hands or paddle. If you don't lean downstream, the current will pile up on the upstream side of your boat and flip you upstream. Exit or roll quickly because the current can wrap the boat around the rock with you inside it, trapping your legs.

If you find yourself caught in a hole, lean the boat downstream into the foam and paddle out the sides.

When swimming in rivers, resist the temptation to stand up in moving water deeper than your knees. Planting your feet on the bottom of the river exposes them to all manner of nasty grabby objects such as undercut rocks, roots, and old automobiles. If your foot becomes entrapped, the

current will push the rest of your body underwater, where it is very hard to breathe. Avoid this situation by lying on your back facing downstream with your feet on the surface, where they can fend off oncoming rocks. To maneuver in this position, point your feet where you don't want to go and angle your head where you do want to go, then backstroke and kick aggressively. If the water is deep enough, turn over on your stomach and swim aggressively to the safest shore.

If you find yourself unavoidably swept into a strainer, abandon the normal feet downstream po-

sition and swim headfirst toward the strainer. Try to climb up on top of the strainer so you pass over it rather than under it.

Unlike the open ocean, where your boat is your ticket to shore, on a river it is not quite as essential to hold onto your boat, although it is usually a good idea if you are not in immediate danger from a downstream hazard. Move upstream of your boat, hold the grab loop and paddle in one hand, and swim toward shore. If you find yourself having to decide between your boat and a sure means of rescuing yourself, rescue yourself first.

Stopping on a River

Eddies Are Your Friends

Because a river is always moving, it is really quite important to know how to stop. You may be approaching the take-out, a campsite, or a rapid you want to take a look at.

Clutching desperately at streamside vegetation is not a recommended way of stopping. Paddling backward will slow your momentum, but you won't be able to stop it for long (I once tried this above a class IV rapid and it didn't work). Turning around and paddling upstream can buy you a bit more time, but you need to have a more permanent solution in mind.

Catching an eddy is the best way to stop on a river. Catching an eddy depends on four crucial factors, all under your control: your kayak's Position, Angle, Lean, and Speed. Think of eddies as your PALS.

Position

Position your boat on the river so you have a straight shot at the top of the eddy where the eddyline is most defined. Kayak A is too far from this eddy and needs to pick an eddy farther downstream. If you keep missing eddies, look farther downstream to give yourself more time to get in position. Kayak D will have to maneuver around the rock and will be pointed in the wrong direction to enter the eddy. Give yourself a clear approach to your eddy. Kayak B looks on target but will be blown downstream by the faster water (this is what usually happens to most new paddlers). Kayak C is pointing at the rock itself to compensate for the fast water just in front of the rock. This is the best position to be in. If you end up actually hitting the rock, congratulate yourself and aim slightly farther down next time.

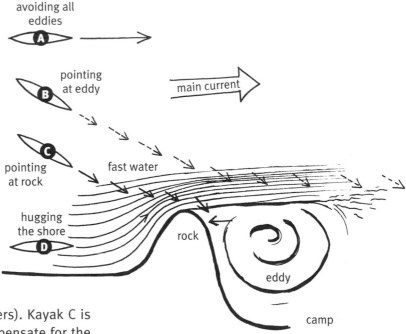

avoiding all eddies

A

pointing at eddy

B

main current

pointing at rock

C

fast water

hugging the shore

D

rock

eddy

camp

Angle

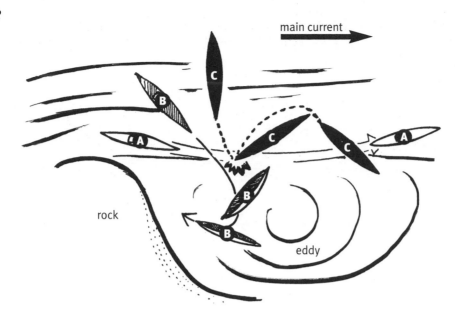

If your approach angle is too shallow relative to the main current (A), you will bounce off the eddyline and continue downstream. A moderate angle (B), will carry you across the eddyline to carve deeply into the eddy. But if your approach angle is *too* steep (C), you will spin out on the eddyline and wash out backward.

Lean

Tilt your boat into the turn as you paddle across the eddyline. You should be able to hold this lean without any paddle support. Hold this lean longer than you think you need to. Keep paddling forward and let the current turn your boat. If you feel particularly unstable you can use a low or high brace on the inside of your turn. Not leaning your boat or stopping your lean while your boat is still turning causes the water moving upstream in the eddy to pile up on your deck and flip you over.

Speed

When in doubt, stroke it out. Eddylines are notoriously unstable places to be, so the faster you go the less time you will spend there. Paddling forward also helps stabilize you. Insufficient speed can result in your boat stalling out and spinning downstream along the eddyline.

What if There's No Eddy?

If there is no eddy in sight, you can still stop by turning upstream and ferrying to shore. It is easier to spin upstream by turning into slower-moving water. Stop your spin when you have a good ferry angle. Look for any micro-eddies or shallow places where you can beach. You can also backpaddle and backferry to shore if you are feeling fancy.

Peel-Outs and Ferries

Peel-Outs

Peeling out is the opposite of catching an eddy but the PALS principles are the same. Look upstream before you head out because boaters coming downstream have the right of way. Position yourself deep in the eddy so you can get your speed up (A).

The angle you exit helps determine your turning radius, so move closer or farther from the eddyline as needed. Just before your bow crosses the eddyline, lean the boat downstream and hold your lean longer than you think you

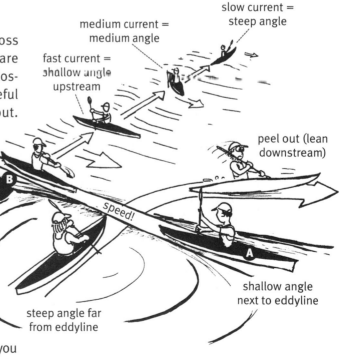

have to (B–C). Keep leaning and paddling forward as you peel out. If you feel particularly unstable you can brace on the downstream side. The greater the difference between your boat speed and the current speed, the greater your lean should be. Stop leaning when you have matched the speed of the current or are facing directly downcurrent (C).

Ferries

Ferrying across rivers is just like ferrying across tidal currents except that the distances are shorter and you can tell right away if you are losing ground. If you leave from an eddy, be careful to keep your ferry from turning into a peel-out. Start next to the eddyline so you have a shallow exit angle, and give yourself enough room to build up speed (A). If you start peeling out, compensate for the force of the current with a stern draw on your downstream side (B). A stern pry on the upstream side will kill your speed, sending you down the river backward. Start ferrying across with a more conservative angle than you think you need and increase it as needed. Point more upstream in fast water and more where you want to go in slower water. If you blow past your campsite, you might be able to paddle back upriver by ferrying between eddies.

Running Rivers

which one to catch?

eddies

must...stay...straight!!

imaginary daggers that Sulu saw in "Day of the Dove" episode #61

A.

B.

My river sense is tingling...

Rumble... Rumble...

C.

D.

E.

F.

Aside from eddy turns, peel-outs, and ferries, running a river is mostly placing your kayak on a line of current that goes where you want to go. Focus far enough downstream so you have time to maneuver as needed (A). Many kayakers have the impression that they always have to point straight downstream (B) but it is okay to be sideways as long as there are no breaking waves or shallow rocks ahead.

The class I and II rapids that touring kayakers should limit themselves to should be easy to run without stopping and scouting. However, if you hear the continuous sound of thunder, see glimpses of white mist splashing above a horizon line, or see other paddlers out of their boats with cameras, you might think about going to shore and scouting (C). Never trust whitewater kayakers who point at a hole and give you the thumbs-up sign. They love carnage even more than board surfers do (G).

Always pull your boat and paddle completely out of the water (D) to avoid any remote-control runs. When scouting, look at the finish where you want to end up and follow lines of current back upstream. Theoretically, if you place your boat on that line at the top you should end up at your destination. Identify distinct landmarks to guide you along the way. Come up with a swim plan in case of a dump (swim to the beach on the left). Before you get back in your boat, crouch down and reidentify your landmarks from a paddler's perspective (E). Remember that it is better to wish you had run a rapid than to wish you had not.

Connect the dots between your landmarks and remember that things come up on you quickly (F).

At the bottom of the rapid (H), smile and reconstruct your run so you can learn from it.

Pee Kayaking

The solution to pollution is dilution.

Staying hydrated and well fed is one of the most important things you can do for your health, but it inevitably leads to peeing and pooping. So what do you do when you are in the middle of the crossing and you have to take a leak? Even more dire, what if you have to poop?

Here are some thoughts to help you turn these previously awkward situations into fun opportunities to test your balance and rescue techniques while having the minimum impact on the environment.

Peeing on dry land, particularly in arid climates, can leave noxious odors for others. It is usually best to pee in the water or below the high-water line. Rivers also have enough flow to dilute urine. Another alternative is to pee on sand or rocks well away from camp or lunch sites. A remarkable number of injuries occur in the middle of the night from people who have to go, so have a flashlight handy or keep a textured plastic bottle in your tent to save yourself a trip.

The number one rule is to go before you have to go. Give yourself plenty of time to get undressed and out of your paddling gear. If you can't escape from your drysuit in time, position yourself and your suit so that you can pee to one side and contaminate only one leg. Accept the fact that whenever you get started other boats will appear out of nowhere and swing by to say hello. If you use TP, pack it out in a resealable bag.

If you can't make it to the loo in time, try the following strategies.

The Drip Dip

Wading into the water during lunch can be the simplest way to relieve yourself. A little swimming and sloshing will help dilute your suit juice. Surfers do this all the time, particularly when they are getting a little chilled. If you have perfected the art of scramble and paddle float rescues, you can treat yourself to an intimate Jacuzzi whenever the need arises. If you are paddling in a tandem boat, your partner can stabilize the boat with a paddle float while you take a dip "to cool off."

The P-Rescue

1.

2.

3.

4.

This is a version of a side rescue that deals with a spill instead of a swim.

1. Have your pee partner bring her bow to your stern and hold onto your cockpit with both paddles across her lap. Pop your skirt and scoot back so you are sitting behind the cockpit with your legs on the seat. Swing both legs into the water. Think warm thoughts. Repeat to yourself: "The water is warmer than it feels."

2. Reach over to your cockpit and turn over onto your stomach so your waist is in the water.

3. Pee. Tell your partner to stop humming the tune to "Jaws."

4. Climb back in your boat as you would for a side rescue. You can also use a paddle float and sling if needed.

Remember to rinse your suit out later. You'll think twice about lending your wetsuit to anyone else. Good soaps for decontaminating wetsuits are "Sink the Stink" and Simple Green.

The Golden Arch (External Plumbing Recommended)

This is a bold move that you have to fully commit to because there's no going back. Before attempting this, build sufficient hydraulic pressure, position yourself on the downwind side, and have a sponge handy to deal with any reentry. Don't forget to pop your sprayskirt.

The Straddle

Scoot out of your seat and straddle the kayak either in front or behind the cockpit, pee freely, and then rinse your lap and legs with water. A very good friend can stabilize your kayak while you do this.

Moon the Fish

The best method for calm conditions is to have a friend hold your paddle and stabilize your boat while you sit on the rear coaming of the cockpit with your feet on your seat. Hold onto your friend's PFD while you pivot your posterior overboard and pee. This maneuver can also be used for emergency bowel movements far from shore.

The Piddle Float

You can do the same maneuver by yourself in calm water with a paddle float and sling. If you can attach your paddle and paddle float to your decklines, the process is much easier. I recommend practicing this in warm, shallow water at first.

1. Take your sling or 12' of line in a loop and drop one end on your leeward side and let your boat drift across the line or use a draw stroke.

2. Pick it up on the other side, and slip the loop over your windward blade.

3. Put your paddle float on your windward blade and inflate it.

4. Place your paddle behind you. Hold onto the other end of the line with your leeward hand the entire time.

5. Move the line to the stern side of your leeward paddle shaft to prevent your paddle from sliding away. You can now safely shift your weight toward your paddle float by maintaining tension on the line with your leeward hand. Scoot your butt out onto the rear deck and place your feet on your seat.

6. Squat and pivot your bottom over the upwind side, holding your cockpit coaming with your other hand. When you are done, reverse the process, keeping tension with your leeward hand. Beware entanglement anytime you use lines.

Bedpans and Beyond

The easiest solution is to pee in your boat. This method is the most stable and you don't have to let anyone else know (although they always find out). Tupperware bedpans, plastic bottles, and plastic baggies can all be used as containers. If you don't have a container, pop your skirt and splash some water on your lap for a rinse. Use your sponge or pump to bail. Finish rinsing out your kayak and bottoms at camp. Avoid this method when tandem paddling.

In a sit-on-top kayak peeing is a no-brainer, but be sure to unplug the scupper stoppers first.

Making Poopies

Hey, it happens. Consider the ability of the local environment to process your poop before someone else finds it or it finds someone else. A proliferation of giardia, a more pristine sense of aesthetics, and a better knowledge of ecological systems have modified techniques. Whichever method you use when moved, be certain to clean your hands thoroughly afterward with soap and water or hand sanitizer.

TP Philosophy

fold

remove corner and save

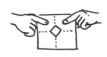

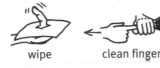
wipe   clean finger

use corner to clean your fingernail

Guide joke on how to use a single sheet of toilet paper: "To conserve TP, we give you one sheet a day." Use this practical joke to break the ice when you give rest-room instructions to your group.

Nothing erodes group morale like a toilet paper shortage. Whether you like to fold or bunch your TP, use reasonable amounts. Always double-bag your TP to keep it dry (even at camp) and always pack it out with you instead of burying it or burning it. If don't have a groover, pack it out in personal sealable baggies doubled up. Feminine hygiene products should also be placed in a lockable baggie that can be placed in the trash or secreted in that person's personals.

To TP or Not to TP?

test

An increasingly popular alternative is to use native material. Don't wait until you arrive at your defecation destination to look for toilet paper options. Start collecting useful items on your way to the chosen place. In scarce country you may have to keep your eyes open throughout the day. My favorite items include water-worked cobbles, seashells, sea weed, overlapped leaves (a basic knowledge of botany is required), snowballs, and smooth sticks. Test objects for texture, temperature, and technique on the inside of your arm.

Go Before You Go

Time your trip to take advantage of previously established rest rooms or outhouses along your route. Beware of drinking too much coffee just before you depart on that 20-mile paddle.

Carry it Out

The next best thing is to carry your waste out with you. Many areas now require paddlers to take along a "groover" or portable toilet system. River rafters pioneered the technique of using army surplus ammo cans, which left telltale grooves in the users' posteriors. Modern systems such as the Boom Box from Ecosafe, WAG Bags from Phillips Environmental Company, or a homemade PVC poop tube (with paper towels for absorbency) are more comfortable and are easier to fit in your kayak. Designate a sign such as a paddle that the user takes with them to show the groover is occupied. Leaving the sign at the groover is unforgivable.

It is critically important not to pee in the groover, otherwise you can run out of space and your system could overflow (always ugly). I have also heard horror stories about groovers exploding from the pressure of ammonia gases in the urine (even uglier). Place the groover close to the water to simplify peeing logistics.

A few drops of bleach, powdered lime, or Knock Out can help neutralize odors. Toilet paper should be the only other item to go in the groover.

At the end of the trip, add some water to loosen things up for easier cleaning. Dispose of all waste appropriately. Never dump any chemically treated waste down trailhead outhouses because the chemicals will destroy the enzyme solution that biodegrades the outhouse waste. The least messy units connect directly to waste dumping facilities at RV parks.

The Subterranean Solution

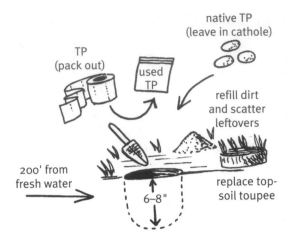

native TP
(leave in cathole)

TP
(pack out)

used
TP

refill dirt
and scatter
leftovers

200' from
fresh water

6–8"

replace top-
soil toupee

The concept of burying your waste for bugs to biodegrade is a sound one if done properly, in areas where there isn't too much use. To reduce the number of land mines around popular camping areas, try to go sometime during the day when you are between campsites where other people are unlikely to visit.

Take a hike well before you start to walk funny. Your cathole will be much more ecologically sound if you are not in a race with your sphincter. Find a place at least 200 feet (70 giant steps) from the nearest water source or wash. If you find a beautiful view where you would hang out if you weren't on a mission, keep walking so you don't mar that site for

someone else. Develop an eye for non-obvious locations where no one else is likely to go.

Use a small trowel to dig up a 6–8 inch diameter toupee of leaf litter and topsoil and set it aside. Continue digging down until your hole is 6–8 inches deep (6 inches can seem quite deep in an emergency). Take the time to place your toilet paper within reach and use any available rocks, logs, or trees to help balance.

The aim game can be interesting, so make sure that you corral any stray doggies with a stick. Place store-bought TP in your sealable baggie and native TP in the hole. Stir some topsoil into the mix for more rapid decomposition. Replace your topsoil toupee and disguise your

site.

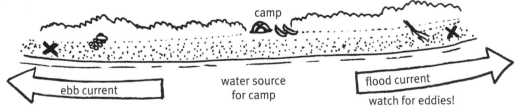

camp

ebb current

water source
for camp

flood current

watch for eddies!

Tidal Stools

The last resort is to poop in the soup. The jury is still out on the effectiveness of this method, but the idea is that wave action, microcritters, and UV light can efficiently break down feces.

The simplest method is to go below the high-tide line where the current will remove the of-

fending material. This location should be close to deep water and far enough from camp to avoid any unpleasant return visits. Be careful of wave action that can surf your scat right back at you. Toss any native TP offshore. Another option is to do your business on a large flat rock that you then hurl offshore (aka "the shitput").

The Log from the Sea of Cortez

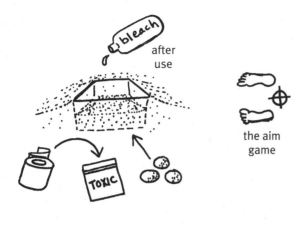

after use

wind

the aim game

If logistics preclude this option, consider doing your business in a plastic container and then transporting it offshore for burial at sea. Choose a plastic container with a lid that is large enough for your needs. Bury it up in the sand and pile sand even with the sides to avoid contaminating the edges. Line the bottom and sides with sand to avoid the aquarium effect. Cover with a well-fitting lid and paddle to a point where the wind or tide will carry it farther from shore. Because your kayak drifts faster downwind than most floating objects, prevent "logjams" by disposing the digested digestibles on the windward side of your kayak. Rinse your container at that time and add a few drops of bleach later to help with odors.

You can also go number two from your boat with the help of a very good friend or a paddle float and sling set up as described on pages 200–201.

A less elegant option is simply to poop while swimming. You can either swim offshore from camp or hold onto your kayak while you go. I am not a fast enough swimmer to try this method with any confidence. Again, making saltwater deposits is not endorsed by the Leave-No-Trace experts but is good to have in your bag of tricks, and preferable to converting your Dagger into a diaper.

Is that a sea slug?

Kayak Camping

"Adventure is not in the guidebook and Beauty is not on the map. Seek and ye shall find."
—TERRY AND RENNY RUSSELL, ON THE LOOSE

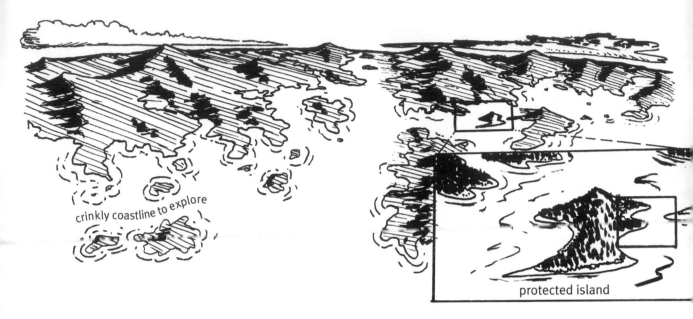

crinkly coastline to explore

protected island

Here's something about pushing off in a kayak loaded for an overnight trip that has the air of a great expedition about it. While kayak camping may not be quite as plush as car camping or river rafting, it seems positively decadent compared to backpacking. Kayak camping is a wonderful way to enjoy yourself even if you are only camping for the night across from your backyard. Exploring your local waterways can be a great way to gain a sense of where you live. At the same time, a paddling adventure to a far-flung destination can improve your paddling skills and experience dramatically.

The Perfect Camp

A. Cove sheltered from wind and waves
B. Early arrival at camp to select the best site and enjoy the good life
C. Previously established campsite on durable terrain
D. Fresh water source a short walk away
E. Bathroom on other side of point
F. Tents and kayaks tucked out of view
G. Kayaks tied and all loose items secured
H. Living room with a view
I. Protected kitchen (cooks only) and tarp for kitchen floor

Choosing Where and When to Go ⌒

I try to plan a warm water paddling trip in the winter and a cool water paddling trip in the summer. Just because a place has been featured on the cover of some adventure magazine doesn't mean it's not worth going to. Even if you do run into some other groups, sea kayakers tend to be pretty amiable folks and may have some extra food to share.

Generally, good sea kayak destinations have crinkly coastlines with endless islands and inlets to explore. If a destination is famous for specific attributes, expect a few disparities. It is hard to find calving glaciers with warm water, protected bays with great surfing, wonderful wildlife with no mosquitoes, and rugged wilderness with easy access.

If crowds annoy you more than mosquitoes, skirt the masses by going in the off seasons or shoulder seasons. Compensate for any inequities by taking more clothes, fresh water, bug spray, or extra time to wait out bad weather. If you have more time than money, you can generally paddle beyond the range of most day paddlers within a few hours. If you have more money than time, you can hire a boat to take you out beyond most other paddlers.

If you decide to explore uncharted waters not referenced (yet) in any guidebook, realize that there will probably be some kinks to work out. This, of course, is what makes it a true adventure.

Keep your group size small to simplify logistics and to minimize your visual and physical impacts. Four is a good number because one can stay with an injured person and two can go for help. Remember to be more conservative than you might be in your backyard bayou. Help may be hours or days away.

Planning Your Route

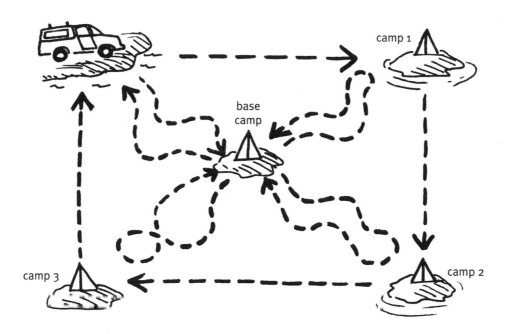

There are two different philosophies for multi-day trips. If you like to cover a lot of coastline you can camp at a new place every night. If you are more apt to mosey you can set up a base camp and go on day trips from there. The best trips are combinations of both paddling and puttering. The average kayaker paddles somewhere around 3 miles an hour, so planning to paddle 12 miles a day is a reasonable estimate after a warm-up day.

If you feel like motoring or if the tide is with you, you can make twenty or more miles a day. If your next planned camp is only three miles away, consider paddling for an extra hour and having a layover day. Use favorable currents and prevailing winds as much as possible and plan some layover days in case of bad weather.

Leave-No-Trace Principles*

- Plan ahead and prepare
- Travel and camp on durable surfaces
- Pack it in, pack it out
- Properly dispose of what you can't pack out
- Leave what you find
- Minimize use and impact of fire
- Respect wildlife
- Be considerate of other visitors

* For more information visit www.LNT.org or call 1-800-332-4100

Camping Gear

I always start packing with my PFD, skirt, boat, paddle, and first-aid kit, and add on from there. I make separate piles for clothes, sleeping gear, kitchen, food, water, safety gear, toiletries, and knickknacks.

Clothes

I always take a rain jacket and rain pants for wind as well as rain. Keep at least one set of clothes, shoes, and socks clean and dry for camp wear. Bring along an empty stuff sack to quarantine clothes that are no longer wearable. Bring a warm hat, a sun hat, and an extra set of Capilene at all times. Consider adding gloves to the list. There may also be room for a comfy cotton shirt and cotton socks to wear in your tent if you really want them and don't ever get them wet.

Sleeping Bags

Down bags are warmest for their weight, but when they get wet they become heavy sponges and lose all their insulation value. If you go on a two-week trip to the rainforests of Southeastern Alaska, I'd recommend a synthetic sleeping bag. Synthetics tend to be bulkier but retain more insulation when wet. To survive sweltering, sticky nights, sew two old cotton sheets together into a sleeping sheet that you can lay on top of your sleeping bag. Use compression sacks to save space but remember to fluff your squished sleeping bag before using it.

Go with a lighter weight bag if you share your tent with a partner who likes to snuggle and is a natural heater. Add a layer if your partner is a cold-footed blanket hog.

psshh!

pull up to tighten
(don't store your
bag like this)

rain jacket

rain paints

clean T-shirt, shorts, and socks for camp

stuff sack for dirty clothes

warm hat

sun hat

warm jacket

warm pants

warm gloves

Sleeping Pads

Invest in a good sleeping pad, particularly if you have joined the ranks of the Ibuprofen Generation. Forget counting ounces and get the thickest one you can, along with a repair kit. The best sleeping pads convert into camp chairs.

Place your sleeping pad or tent on a groundcloth to minimize punctures and help keep things dry. If the ground is broiling hot, splash water on the ground before you lay down your groundcloth.

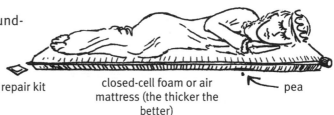

repair kit

closed-cell foam or air mattress (the thicker the better)

pea

Tarps and Tents

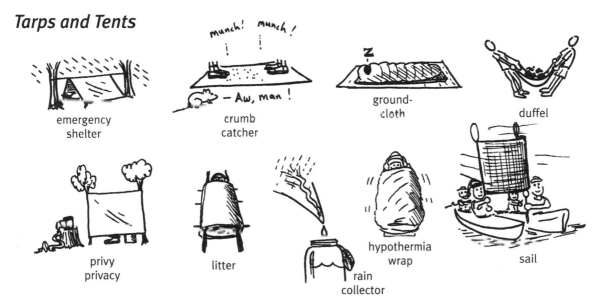

munch! munch!

— Aw, man!

emergency shelter

crumb catcher

groundcloth

duffel

privy privacy

litter

rain collector

hypothermia wrap

sail

You should be able to set up your tent in the dark in a squall without a flashlight, because that is what happens anyway. Seal the seams of your tent, tent fly, and tarps before the trip.

Bring along an extra tarp or two, but leave the unwieldy blue PVC monster tarp at home. Tarps have dozens of uses: a rain shelter for the kitchen crew, a crumb catcher on burrito night, a groundcloth, luggage cart to and from kayaks, a privacy curtain, an emergency litter, a rainwater funnel, an outer wrap for a hypothermic person, or a makeshift sail on a downwind day.

"Can I borrow your flashlight to find my flashlight?"

headnet · lighter · skull cap · hand sanitizer · sunscreen · lip balm · water purification tablets · head-lamp · knife or multitool

film canister tooth-brush protector

cut hole in lid

fanny pack

use screw-tight lids instead of fliplids, and double-bag oozables

Keeping track of gear is a daunting task until you figure out a system. I keep small essentials in a fanny pack, which I store in my day hatch in my boat. The items I have found indispensable include a headnet, bug repellent, lighter, skull cap, hand sanitizer, sunscreen, lip balm, water purification tablets, small flashlight, and knife. Use screw-tight lids instead of flip-top lids on oozable items like toothpaste, moisturizer, and sunscreen. Pack a strainer or some foldable window screen material to strain food particles from your wastewater.

Invite a gearhead to bring amenities that you would never bring yourself but don't mind using. These extras include solar showers, cushy camp chairs, hammocks, and espresso makers. Other useful items that you might not think of at first include a deck of cards, binoculars and a bird book, a frisbee or hacky sack, and a good book. I recommend *Endurance* by Alfred Lansing, *The River Why* by David James Duncan, *West with the Night* by Beryl Markham, and, of course, *Harry Potter and the Sorcerer's Stone* by J.K. Rowling.

Leave the following items at home: your palm pilot, a 6-pound roll of duct tape, a roll of paper towels, extra cotton clothing, your float plan, saws and hatchets, and your worries.

double-bagged (slide locks don't work well with powder)

directions

Kayaking Cuisine

Don't plan on losing weight during a sea kayaking trip. There's room to bring all types of yummy meals and lots of snacks to eat throughout the day. You don't have to limit yourself to eating classic GORP fare (Gorp, Oatmeal, Ramen, and Peanut Butter) and can think instead of Gnocchi, Omelets, Risotto, and Pancakes. For longer trips, when you cannot carry fresh fruits and veggies for the entire time, consider drying them. Dehydrators do not take long to pay for themselves considering the cost of commercially available dried fruits and veggies.

Transfer food from bulky packages to collapsible plastic baggies. Cut out cooking directions and place them inside the baggies, and double-bag potentially messy items such as brownie mix, hot cocoa, and cooking oil. Include a few extra Cup-a-Soup meals in case your trip is unintentionally extended or someone becomes hypothermic. Remove the labels of any cans (they disintegrate when wet) and write the contents on the lid with a permanent marker. Packets of condiments from fast-food restaurants are more camp-friendly than larger containers. Make sure that the person responsible for packing breakfasts is a coffee drinker. Keep healthy by washing or sanitizing your hands frequently.

Water, Water, Everywhere . . .

Always filter, purify, iodize, or boil water and have a backup method on hand. Something is always pooping higher than you. Plan on using one gallon of water per person per day and ration fresh water accordingly. Collapsible plastic water jugs are great space savers. Water bottles are easier to refill on camping trips than fancy hydration systems. When cooking pasta, save your fresh water by boiling a mixture of half fresh water and half salt water.

Packing

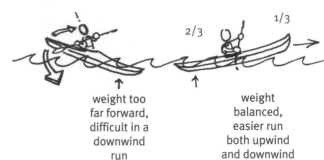

Plan launching and landing at high tides to avoid long walks. Bring a duffel bag to transfer your gear between shuttles, kayaks, and camp. Use your significant other or rollers to help you transport the heavy stuff. Don't load your kayak until it is partly supported by water. Scoot your kayak up and down as the tide changes so you don't end up beached or boatless.

Several small drybags are more useful than one large one because they can fit through small hatches and into tight nooks. If you have a large drybag, you may have to place it inside the kayak before filling it and keep enough of the top out to seal it effectively. Stay organized by using differently colored drybags that are consistently packed with the same gear. Line your drybags with lawn or trash compactor garbage bags. If you are on a budget, you can create low-budget drybags by lining stuff sacks with garbage bags.

Start loading by placing small bags in small places and skinny bags in skinny spaces. Tie a string to small stuff sacks to retrieve them without assuming advanced yoga positions. For most paddling conditions, distribute one-third of the weight in the bow and two-thirds in the stern. Pack the heaviest objects low and securely along the centerline directly behind your

weight too far forward, difficult in a downwind run

2/3 **1/3**

weight balanced, easier run both upwind and downwind

seat. If weathercocking or broaching is a problem, shift more weight to the stern to give the stern a better bite on the water.

Stash your warm hat, paddling jacket, and first-aid kit in the same easy, accessible place in the same stuff sacks throughout the trip. Don't store anything between your knees that can inhibit your ability to wet exit. Everything leftover goes on the deck, so make sure these items are both waterproof and well secured. Minimize deck debris, because these items are easily lost and interfere with rescues and rolling.

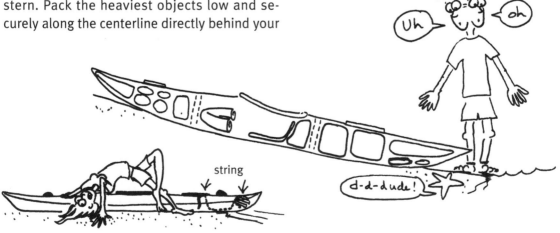

string

Uh oh

d-d-dude!

Campsite Selection

Start looking for campsites well before dark so you have time to find a good camp and enjoy it in the daylight. Check in with other groups to find out where they are camping so you avoid camping on top of each other. If there is competition for campsites, direct the conversation in your favor by announcing where you plan to camp first. Before you camp next to another party, be a good neighbor and check in with them before unloading your boats. They might know of another great place just around the corner. If you have only two people in your group, don't occupy a large camp better suited for twenty.

Silence is one of the most precious resources out there. Sounds travel much farther than you might expect, so be mindful of your group's noise level.

Always try to use a previously established campsite. If none is available, select a site on sand, gravel, or bedrock instead of on vegetation. If there's no bare ground, set your tent up on resilient annuals such as grasses and avoid woody shrubs. Place your camp and kayaks far enough from shore to preserve a pristine view for others, but don't bushwhack a highway to a tent site a quarter mile from the water.

how campsite sprawl starts

Making Yourself at Home

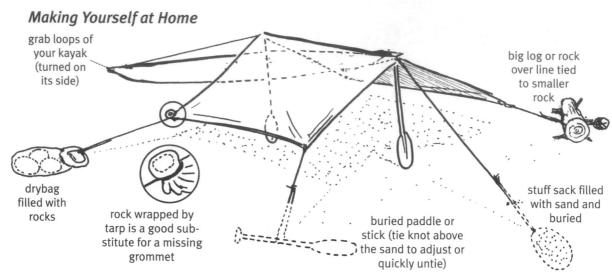

grab loops of your kayak (turned on its side)

big log or rock over line tied to smaller rock

drybag filled with rocks

rock wrapped by tarp is a good substitute for a missing grommet

buried paddle or stick (tie knot above the sand to adjust or quickly untie)

stuff sack filled with sand and buried

Select your home with natural windbreaks and solar heating in mind. Sleep out under the stars whenever you can, but have your tent handy in case of midnight showers or heavy dew. Avoid sleeping under cottonwood trees, coconut trees, and the bases of cliffs to avoid being bonked. Tarps and tents are happiest out of the wind on raised or sloping terrain. Depressions make them depressed. Tuck the edges of your groundcloth under your tent so it doesn't turn into a wetland, and stake out your fly so it doesn't touch the tent wall. Digging moats around your tent is now considered bad form and is unnecessary with good tent placement.

You can convert your tarp into a spiffy shelter with enough parachute cord, bowlines, tautline hitches, and props (see the Carrying Kayaks chapter). Secure the tarp low to the ground so it doesn't turn into a spinnaker, and support it so it doesn't turn into natatorium.

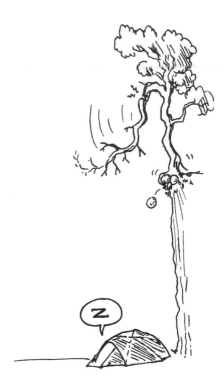

groundcloth funnels water into tent

groundcloth tucked underneath tent

"Fire! Heh, Heh! Fire!"—Beavis

Whenever possible, reduce your impact by using a camping stove instead of a fire. You will have unobstructed views of the stars, won't have to dodge smoke, and won't have to take the time for messy cleanups. In addition, fires and firewood gathering may be illegal or restricted in some places. Check local fire regulations and conditions before you go.

If you just can't resist having a fire and conditions permit, build one that won't sterilize the soil, scar rocks, or leave any other trace.

Use a previously established fire ring if possible. Break the cycle of filling one fire ring with broken bottles and trash and constructing another beside it. Clean up any Budweiser boneyards and disperse duplicate rings.

fire ring

If there aren't any fire rings, bring a small oil pan or roasting pan to contain your fire. Balance the pan on rocks to protect the soil underneath.

fire pan on rocks

If you don't have a fire pan you can still build a mound fire. Place a tarp on the ground and pile enough sand or mineral soil (6–8") on top to insulate the tarp from the fire. Return the sand to its source once you have cleaned up the fire.

Another option is to build your fire in a shallow hole in the sand below the high-tide or high-

mound fire

water mark (check your tide table and local regulations first!).

pit fire (check tide table)

The best leave-no-trace fire is the flashlight fire. Place your clear water jug on top of a headlight so the light shines up through the water. Shine a headlamp through a Nalgene water bottle for the candle lantern version.

Start collecting firewood before dark far enough from camp so you don't denude your neighborhood. Select dead and downed driftwood smaller than your wrist so it burns completely. Gather more tinder and kindling than you think you'll need. Resist the temptation to burn one end of a giant log, leaving an ugly stump as your legacy. Impress your friends with your command over the elements by using some fire starter sticks or fire ribbon.

Stoke the fire to burn all wood to ash. Designate a responsible person to drown the fire before going to bed. The next morning dig up and pack out any solid bits of charcoal with your trash. Cold ashes can be carried out with your trash, or strained and dispersed on land away from camp. In some heavy-sediment, high-volume rivers you can strain and sift ashes into the current. Scatter any unused kindling and firewood or take it with you to the next camp. Finish by disguising your fire site.

scatter cold ashes on land away from camp

or

pack out all solids and ashes

trash

dead fire (cool to touch)

or sift and swim ashes and pack out solids (check local regulations)

Camp Life

Windproof your camp by securing all your gear to something heavier. Tents, hatch covers, sleeping pads, drybags, and PFDs can easily sail away in an unexpected gust.

Always wear shoes in camp. A punctured sole and bruised toe can ruin your whole trip. Bring your headlamp to dinner with you and to midnight potty runs.

Take advantage of sunlight and wind to dry out your secured gear. After the sun sets you can still dry out damp objects by sleeping with them and letting your body heat dry them.

Cleaning

Save your drinking water supply by using sea, river, or lake water for dishwashing. Use hot water and, if needed, a minimal amount of biodegradable soap. Strain all wastewater through a screen and pack out the solid bits in your trash. If you are along the ocean or a high-volume, high-sediment river, you can pour the strained water back into the water. In most freshwater settings move 200' from the water and scatter it. Sterilize your cookware and utensils in boiling water or with a very dilute bleach solution. Stay healthy by not sharing bowls or mugs with other people.

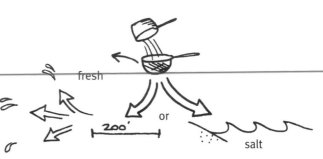

fresh

or

salt

strain and scatter 200' from fresh water

strain and swim in salt water

Megatrash and Microtrash

Megatrash is the deathly cold, gray blob of oatmeal that no one ate. Microtrash consists of crumbs, twist ties, bread bag tabs, and even sunflower seed shells. Pack all of it out, even your biodegradable, wildlife-edible, and perfectly natural apple cores. Any organic matter can attract ants, scorpions, mice, snakes and the rest of the food chain to this site. Reduce your microtrash by carefully choosing the types of food you bring, eating drippy meals over the water, lining your kitchen floor with a tarp and sweep-

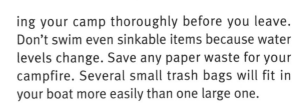

ing your camp thoroughly before you leave. Don't swim even sinkable items because water levels change. Save any paper waste for your campfire. Several small trash bags will fit in your boat more easily than one large one.

Windbound!
or When You Want to Leave But Can't

"It is better to be here wishing you were out there than out there wishing you were back here."

You wake up and what you hoped had been your tent mate's snoring really is a Force 8 gale. Paddling is impossible, so what do you do? First, accept your situation and adjust your attitude accordingly. Forget the big contract at work or the international flight you're missing and turn a windbound day into a relaxing layover day. Be optimistic and check the weather, boats, and tent frequently. Read a good book aloud, write in your journal, play hacky sack, or go for a hike. You know that "pshhh!" sound a cold beer makes when you crack it open? Well, don't think about it now.

Wake up early the next morning to take advantage of any breaks in the weather but don't expect to make twenty miles. Plan on several closer camps if the weather worsens again once you get back on the water.

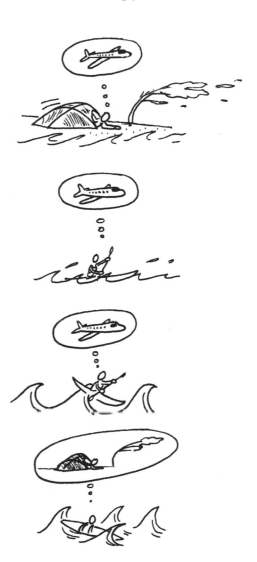

Special Topics

"Da dum. Da dum. Da dum, da dum, da dum . . ."
—JOHN WILLIAMS' THEME TO "JAWS"

*T*his chapter is devoted to elements beyond winds and waves that kayakers need to be aware of: critters, lightning, icebergs, and hypothermia.

Critters

One of the reasons to kayak is to see critters you wouldn't otherwise see. Of course this means that these critters don't normally see you. Marine mammals already have enough to worry about without adding kayaking paparazzi to their list of grievances. The Marine Mammal Protection Act is designed to give these critters some much-needed privacy. The Act prohibits you from changing an animal's behavior, meaning you should keep a minimum distance of 100 yards from whales, seals, sea lions, and dolphins. You can still trigger a stampede of seals into the water from farther distances, so carry binoculars for close views.

What if the critter hasn't read the regulations and approaches you? Enjoy the encounter, but maintain a minimum distance to prevent physical contact. You may have to stop paddling forward or even paddle away from it. Use your paddle to discourage overly aggressive sharks, snakes, gators, and geese. Curious seals will follow behind you and dive underwater when you turn your head. If you suspect a sneaky seal is following you and want a better look, paddle backward.

Seals and Sea Lions

seal—easily scared

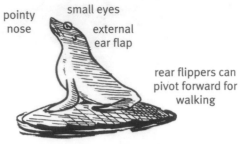

sea lion—males are territorial

Seals are much more skittish on land than in the water. When a hauled-out seal raises its head up, it is a red light telling you to back off. If the seal lays its head back down, cautiously proceed, giving it a wider berth. If the seal doesn't lower its head, back up and try a different route.

Sea lion bulls can defend their territory quite aggressively. When you see a big male "greet" you, back off. Staring or pointing your boat directly at an animal is regarded as an act of aggression, so avert your eyes as you retreat. Always give animals on shore or docks plenty of room to reach the water without belly flopping on you.

Sea Otters, Sea Cows, Dugongs, and Manatees

Sea otters were almost exterminated by Aleutian kayakers working for Russian fur traders, so avoid any more bad kayak karma by respecting their space. Sea cows and their kin are gentle, shy, and extremely endangered, so be gentle and shy with them.

Hairy P. Otter

Whales

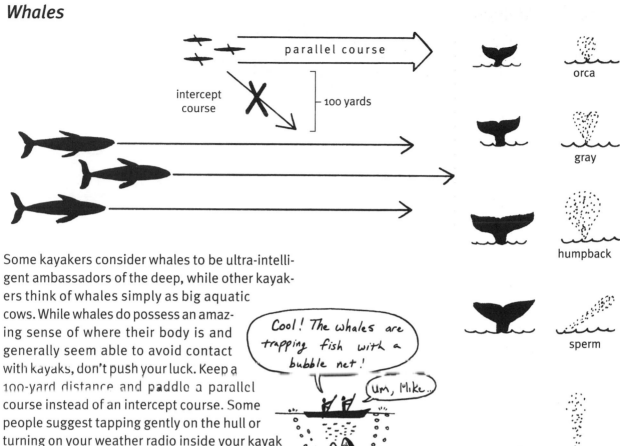

parallel course

intercept course

100 yards

orca

gray

humpback

sperm

blue

Some kayakers consider whales to be ultra-intelligent ambassadors of the deep, while other kayakers think of whales simply as big aquatic cows. While whales do possess an amazing sense of where their body is and generally seem able to avoid contact with kayaks, don't push your luck. Keep a 100-yard distance and paddle a parallel course instead of an intercept course. Some people suggest tapping gently on the hull or turning on your weather radio inside your kayak so whales can better sense your presence and location. Just hope that your tapping doesn't arouse their curiosity or annoy them. Gray whales are known to be particularly ornery toward kayakers.

I hold baby whales in the same category as baby grizzly bears. Mothers can be very protective and may view your kayak as a shark-like predator, while the young may view your kayak simply as a bathtub toy.

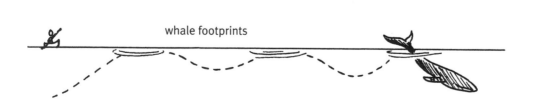

whale footprints

Sharks and Rays

Life is always more interesting in the middle of the food chain. Even though you have a better chance of dying in a unicycle crash on your way to the beach than being attacked by a shark, few concepts are more disconcerting than being eaten by a prehistoric fish. Avoid paddling near well-known shark supermarkets such as marine mammal colonies. Paddle with a partner so you have another boat to climb on if a shark bites and sinks your boat.

Stingrays are innocuous enough until you step on them and they stab you with the spike at the base of their tail. Shoo them off when wading in shallow salt water by walking slowly and shuffling your feet along the bottom.

Snakes

Most snakes will move out of your way, but some species, such as the water moccasin in the southeastern United States, are more aggressive and will chase you out of their territory. If a snake falls from an overhanging branch and lands on your head, find some small comfort that this is an escape mechanism and not an attack. Always pay attention where you place your hands or feet on shore.

Crocodiles and Kin

Alligators, caimans, and crocodiles are usually quite shy but there are always stories of sneak snack attacks. Ask local kayakers or fishermen if there are any places you should avoid.

Bears

Paddling in bear country means you have to be smarter than your average bear when you make camp. You can also camp on really small islands and hope that the bears don't feel like swimming. Always keep your bear spray handy.

Avoid bears by picking well-kept campsites and keeping your campsite squeaky clean. Set up your kitchen a few minutes' walk downwind from camp. Find a separate place a few minutes farther on to stash your food, sunscreen, toothpaste, cook clothes, and soap.

Bear-proof containers are wonderful items and should be taken anytime you travel in bear country. Pick a container from a backpacking store that fits easily in your kayak. Don't try to convince yourself that your waterproof hatch is also bear-proof. Bears think that kayaks are simply the plastic toy that comes with the happy meal. Even if you have bear-proof containers, you should still stash your food away from camp.

If you don't have a bear-proof container and do have enough rope, tall trees, time, and perseverance, you can hang your food. To get started, stuff rocks in a stuff sack, tie it to a rope, and toss it over a strong, high branch. There are many variations from there. Hanging food is notoriously hazardous work, so consider wearing a helmet to ward off misfired rocks and broken branches. If hanging your food isn't an option, make a few food caches far from camp and hope for the best. Some folks even store their food in the hatches and anchor the kayak offshore.

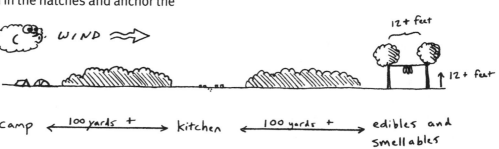

Raccoons, Ringtails, and Rodents

These industrious critters will chew through tents, stuff sacks, and water bottles to get to food and then poop on everything else. Aside from bear-proof containers, your closed kayak hatch may be the best storage area for your food as long as you are not in bear country. Don't forget your energy bar in your PFD pocket or you may find a non-Coast Guard approved modification in the morning. Avoid sleeping under overhangs and other "Hanta houses" where rodents and their deadly viruses abound.

Birds

Unless you want to say "Never more" to your bagel, don't turn your back on your lunch when ravens are about. Ravens and gulls can carry off unattended items and can tear camps apart. Camp security aside, take the time to learn a few of your backwater birds. A kayak is a wonderful bird-watching vehicle, particularly if you have a rudder and can steer while looking through binoculars. Keep your distance to avoid disturbing colonies of nesting birds, many of which have migrated enormous distances to be there. Dive bombing and screeching are good indications that you are too close. Avoid walking on upper beaches where shorebirds have hidden their eggs.

Mosquitoes and Other Nuisances

In this case the food you are trying to protect is yourself. Start by selecting camps or kitchens in windy areas away from marshes and mangroves. A headnet can be invaluable, but remember to lift it up when eating and brushing teeth. Wear a headnet over a hat with brim to keep the mesh off your face. Long-sleeved shirts, pants, socks, and gloves complete the picture. DEET is a very effective deterrent, but it

bowl buried in sand

can also melt your plastic boat. Minimize your contact with it by using a stick form. Premethria works well on clothes (not skin) if pre-applied before your trip. Thoroughly search your tent before you go to bed at night, lest you wake up to one really fat mosquito. To displace swarms of gnats, hold your hat above your head.

If your campsite suffers from an ant invasion, bury several bowls or containers lip-deep in the sand to serve as ant traps. Release them when you leave. Scorpions like to hide underneath flat objects, so sleep on a tarp to give them a hiding place other than under your sleeping bag. Shake out your booties in the morning to dislodge earwigs and spiders.

An arthropod's guide to human behavior

Stowaways

Stored kayaks make great homes for earwigs, black widow spiders, centipedes, and wood rats. If you did not store your kayak with the cockpit covered, you may want to flush out uninvited guests with a hose or slosh your boat out at the ramp before you seal yourself in.

Ecologically disastrous invasive species such as zebra mussels and Eurasian milfoil often hitchhike in boats as babies. Hose your boat and gear out before paddling in new areas.

Lightning

Since you have a greater chance of being struck by lightning than being eaten by a shark, you should be looking up more often than down. Learn your local weather patterns, listen to your weather radio, keep an eye on the sky, and have emergency bail-out points in mind. Lightning strikes most commonly at the leading edge of a storm, so seek shelter on shore before it starts to rain. When a lightning strike is a mile away, there will be a five-second delay between the flash and the boom. Once on shore, spread your group out so that if someone is directly or indirectly struck by lightning, there will be someone else who can offer first aid. Crouch down on top of your PFD to keep a low profile and minimize your contact with the ground. Hypothermia is often a concern at this point as well.

Glaciers and Icebergs

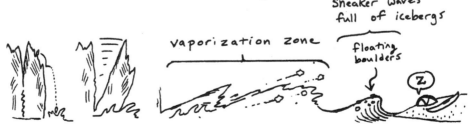

Paddling around glaciers and icebergs is one of the coolest things you can do, but paddle conservatively to avoid ending up blended or on the rocks. Seemingly stable icebergs regularly and unpredictably roll over as the ice below the surface melts away. Faces of glaciers can collapse, or worse, fall forward, creating a cannonball effect far beyond your expectations. The waves created by calving icebergs can wreak havoc on normally surfless beaches, particularly if there are icebergs along the shoreline. Steady winds can squeeze bergy bits together and pinch out open-water leads, so keep an eye on the weather and go around the floe.

Haplessthermia

More than sneaky sharks or boat-bashing icebergs, hypothermia is the number one hazard for kayakers. Hypothermia is a dangerous and potentially deadly lowering of a body's core temperature. I also call this condition "haplessthermia," because hypothermia affects the judgment centers of your brain, effectively lowering your intelligence, altering your personality, and interfering with your ability to take care of yourself. Normally savvy paddlers start making navigational errors, taking unnecessary risks, and missing rolls. Seemingly minor mistakes quickly spiral out of control with tragic results. Hypothermia occurs not just from immersion in cold water, but more often from prolonged exposure to surprisingly mild conditions both in kayaks and in camp. The classic stage for hypothermia is a breezy, drizzly 55° day. The classic victim is tired, hungry, didn't bring enough warm clothes because it's not particularly cold, and is too preoccupied with getting to shore or setting up the tent to put on a hat.

Prevention and Treatment

Ward off hypothermia by anticipating changing conditions, wearing a hat, eating and drinking to feed your metabolism, and keeping active. Put another layer on as soon as the wind picks up or when you stop for lunch, before you start feeling cold. Early symptoms include acting spacey, grouchy, or apathetic, and being unable to perform simple tasks like finding a campsite on a huge sandy beach.

To treat a hypothermic paddler, put a hat on his head, land at a safe shore, and help him out of his kayak. Dry him off while minimizing his exposure to the elements and dress him in warm, dry clothes. Next, mummify him in a warm sleeping bag surrounded by a space blanket, sleeping pad, and a tarp. Give him some quick-energy food and take the time to make a hot drink for him if he can drink it himself. A hot water bottle in the hands or groin can help his attitude. Be extremely gentle with incapacitated hypothermic patients, as jarring them can cause heart attacks. Seek medical help as soon as you stabilize them. Don't become hypothermic yourself by neglecting your own needs or lending all your own warm clothes away.

Index